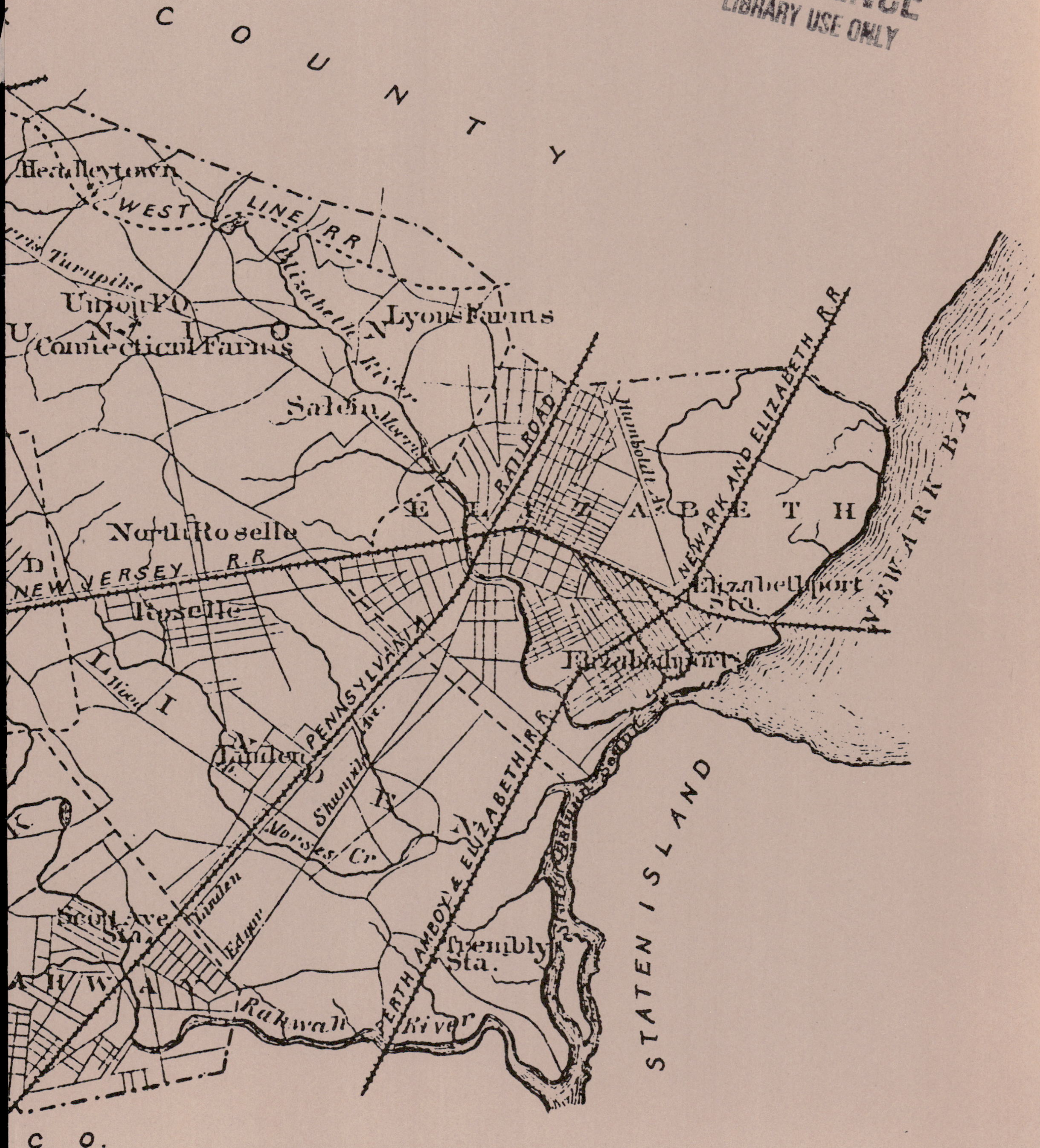
COUNTY
WEST LINE RR
Turnpike
Union P.O.
Connecticut Farms
Lyons Farms
Elizabeth River
Salem
RAILROAD
NEWARK AND ELIZABETH R.R.
ELIZABETH
NEWARK BAY
North Roselle
NEW JERSEY R.R.
Roselle
Elizabethport Sta.
Elizabethport
PENNSYLVANIA
Linden
PERTH AMBOY & ELIZABETH R.R.
Morses Cr
STATEN ISLAND
Sta.
Rahway River
C O.

Elizabethtown & Union County
A Pictorial History

by Charles L. Aquilina, Richard T. Koles, and Jean-Rae Turner

Charles L. Aquilina
Richard T. Koles
Jean-Rae Turner

THE NATIONAL STATE BANK
Offices throughout New Jersey.

A limited edition of 1,500 of which this is number 38.

*The National State Bank
is proud to present
this pictorial history
of Elizabethtown & Union County*

*The success
we have experienced since
our bank was established in 1812
is due in large measure
to the support of our friends
in Union County*

*Therefore, we dedicate
this book to
the citizens of Union County*

Elizabethtown & Union County
a Pictorial History

Charles L. Aquilina, Richard T. Koles,
and Jean-Rae Turner

Design by Jamie Backus Raynor
Donning Company/Publishers
Norfolk/Virginia Beach

*To all who love and enjoy history in the
hope that they will continue to inspire others.*

Copyright © 1982
   by Charles L. Aquilina, Richard T. Koles,
     and Jean-Rae Turner

All rights reserved, including the right to
reproduce this work in any form whatsoever
without permission in writing from the
publisher, except for brief passages in
connection with a review. For information write:
The Donning Company/Publishers
5659 Virginia Beach Boulevard
Norfolk, Virginia 23502

Library of Congress Cataloging in Publication Data

Aquilina, Charles L., 1916-
   Elizabethtown and Union County.

   Bibliography: p.
   Includes index.
   1. Union County (N. J.)—History—Pictorial works.
2. Union County (N. J.)—Description and travel—Views.
3. Elizabeth (N. J.)—Description—Views. 4. Elizabeth
(N. J.)—History—Pictorial works. I. Koles, Richard T.,
1927- II. Turner, Jean-Rae, 1920-
III. Title.
  F142.U5A68   1982   974.9'36   82-12939
  ISBN 0-89865-271-5

Printed in the United States of America

CONTENTS

Foreword 6
Preface 7
Introduction 9
Chapter I
   In the Beginning 1492-1664 13
Chapter II
   Out of the Wilderness—
   Elizabethtown 1664-1775 25
Chapter III
   Elizabethtown—Gateway to
   the Revolution 1775-1800 35
Chapter IV
   Trails to Trains 1785-1865 49
Chapter V
   Great Expectations 1865-1900 59
Chapter VI
   Americans All 103
Chapter VII
   Into the Twenty-first
   Century 1900-Present 133
Acknowledgments 218
Bibliography 219
Index 220

FOREWORD

n anniversary is usually a time for celebration. But it should be more. It should also be a time for reflection, for looking back, for taking stock. It is especially fitting, therefore, that the 125th anniversary of Union County be commemorated with the publication of this revealing picture history.

Although Union is the youngest of New Jersey's twenty-one counties, the area that it encompasses has had a rich and sometimes stormy history reaching back into the colonial period. This volume covers the full sweep of that colorful story, from the time that the sails of European ships first appeared off the Jersey shore down to the present day.

The approaches to history are many and varied. This work is, essentially, a history told through pictures—like a Union County family album. But it is not an exercise in nostalgia. The artist's brush and the camera's lens have their own perceptions. Thus, the pictures on the following pages tell their own truths and capture, often more eloquently than words, the look and texture of the past.

The authors came to this work from equally distinguished careers: one as an educator, one as a journalist, and the third as a professional photographer. They share a deep interest in a knowledge of the county's history. The authors' task was not an easy one; but they did their work wisely and well. Drawing on the resources of private collections, libraries, and local historical societies, they have created this extraordinary gallery of pictures, most of which are published here for the first time.

Finally, it must be recognized that this work represents an even wider collaboration than that of the authors, for it took the efforts of many men and women, artists and photographers to create and preserve for us this remarkable record of our heritage. To each of these contributors, many long forgotten, we owe our thanks.

Robert Fridlington, President
Union County Historical Society
and Professor of History at
Kean College of New Jersey, Union
April 13, 1982

PREFACE

nion County possesses a long and distinguished history. It is still one of the most diverse areas in New Jersey, encompassing large cities and suburban communities.

Elizabethtown, the county seat, was the site of the first English government in New Jersey. It was later the original capital of the new state of New Jersey.

During the nineteenth century, Union County's towns were in the forefront of America's industrial revolution, and they continue that tradition today, housing some of the most advanced modern industries such as computer technologies and telecommunications.

Union County is also very diverse ethnically. Immigrants from around the world have made their homes here, starting in the seventeenth century, and their various heritages have contributed greatly to the culture of the area.

Union County is an interesting place, a microcosm mirroring many of the trends in New Jersey and in the United States. I am pleased to recommend the contents of this volume to all readers.

Thomas H. Kean
Governor

The seal of Union County, New Jersey, depicts the murder of Hannah Ogden Caldwell on June 7, 1780, by a British or Hessian soldier after the Battle of Connecticut Farms. Mrs. Caldwell, wife of the pastor of the Elizabethtown Presbyterian Church, was staying in the parsonage of the Connecticut Farms Presbyterian Church. She refused to take refuge beyond First Mountain when the soldiers aproached. After the shooting, Mrs. Caldwell's body was carried to the Wade farmhouse nearby, and the parsonage was burned. Photograph by Richard T. Koles

*Those Who Labor in Earth
are the Chosen People*
—Thomas Jefferson

This pastoral scene of Springfield in 1907 was typical of much of Union County until after World War II. There were still 200 farms plus 53 dairy farms listed in Union County in the late 1950s. By the early 1970s, fewer than ninety farms with ten acres or more each were listed, and only three dairy farms were left. In 1982 the county boasted a single milk distribution company, the Tuscan Dairy Company in Union Township, and all of their cows were gone. Photograph from a postcard; courtesy of Betty Olson, Roselle Public Library

The Gideon Ross farm, later known as the Ripley home, was located on Elizabeth Avenue, Westfield. Photograph courtesy of the Westfield Historical Society

INTRODUCTION

*Nothing is aimed at more than a
fair and candid representation*
Samuel Smith

nion County, youngest of New Jersey's twenty-one counties and the second smallest, contains the state's oldest English-speaking community, Elizabeth, settled in 1664, and some of the state's oldest historic sites. The county's formation on March 19, 1857, from the southern portion of Essex County ended more than 190 years of political bickering for leadership between Essex County's two major communities, Elizabethtown and Newark Town, settled in 1666.

In the early days of the colony of New Jersey, the courthouse was located in Elizabethtown. After it was moved to Newark Town, the people in Elizabethtown wanted it returned to them. A union of people in the southern part of Essex County urged the separation. Finally in 1807, a referendum was held between Newark Town and a compromise site, Day's Hill (former location of Olympic Park, the amusement park), in Irvington. Historians describe the election as the most crooked ever held in the state. Men, women and blacks, including slaves, voted many times. Newark won the election. Elizabethtown denounced the election as a fraud. The election was set aside. A second election was held, and the courthouse remained in Newark.

In the dispute that followed, women and blacks lost the vote. Blacks regained it after the Civil War, but women had to wait until 1920. The dispute sowed the seeds of discontent and the desire for independence from Newark.

After Elizabeth became a city in 1855, Mayor Elias Darby started a movement which culminated with the final break from Essex County two years later. Moses Miller Crane, who is called the Father of Union County, suggested the unusual name. Since the separation occurred on the eve of the Civil War, Crane may have selected the word because of common concern

9

The first Summit railroad station, circa 1890. Photograph courtesy of the Newark Public Library

for the Union or perhaps because of the informal union of people who had earlier attempted to form an independent county.

The new county contained 103.4 square miles. It was completely in the Piedmont Plains area. Low ridges of the Watchung Mountains extended along its western boundary, the Passaic River. Except for valleys between First and Second mountains, the land slopes from the highest point 553 feet above sea level (now Tip Top Way, Berkeley Heights) to sea level.

The new county was sparsely settled. It had only 25,000 people. More than half of these resided in Elizabeth, where small industries were active in Elizabethport. The new county also included Westfield, formed on January 17, 1794; Springfield, April 14, 1794; Rahway, February 27, 1804; Union Township, November 23, 1808; New Providence, 1809; and Plainfield, 1847.

The boundaries included all of Elizabethtown before it was whittled down by inhabitants successfully forming their own communities. The boundaries between Middlesex and Morris counties were the same as they had been between Essex and those counties. The boundary between the new county and Essex County was unsettled until March 17, 1882. Originally the boundary between Elizabethtown and Newark Town had been Bound Creek to Divident Hill and up the Road to Lyon's Farms (Lyons Avenue, Newark). The present line is about half a mile south of that line. It continued the division of Lyon's Farms between Union and Clinton townships, slashed through Hilton and caused a new community, Millburn, to be formed from Springfield (until 1794 called the spring fields), when it placed half of that township in the new county and left half in Essex County.

Union County was ideally located at the crossroads of a corridor state. Three major railroads passed through it, and others were being planned to cut through the Watchung Mountains. It was situated on the major highways of the day—the Old York Road, the King's Highway, and the Morris Turnpike.

Ferries plied between Elizabethport and New York City just twelve miles away. The easy access to New York City and the excellent train service was already causing residential development in Westfield, Cranford, Plainfield, Elizabeth, Rahway and the Summit. ■

This view of the central part of Elizabeth City on Saturday, May 31, 1856, shows the railroad tracks before the Arch was built. Photograph courtesy of the Elizabeth Public Library

View of Main Street, Rahway, circa 1857. From Charles L. Aquilina's collection; photograph by Richard T. Koles

The courthouse and the Presbyterian church in Elizabeth are shown circa 1857 separated by the Liberty Pole in the center. Photograph courtesy of the Elizabeth Public Library

View of Elizabethport with the United States steamship, Dispatch in the foreground, May 1889. Photograph courtesy of the Elizabeth Public Library

England's claim to the American continent is based on voyages by John Cabot and his son Sebastian (shown here). Photograph from Benson J. Lossing's The Pictorial Field-Book of the Revolution

Giovanni da Verrazano, a Florentine navigator employed by France, claimed the New Jersey area as New France in 1524. The bridge between Staten Island and Brooklyn was named in his honor. Upon his return to France, he reported "fertile fields for agriculture" and "natives wearing bird feathers.... They came toward us with evident delight raising loud shouts of admiration and showed us where we could securely land our boats" (Hagaman, Early New Jersey). *Photograph from Benson J. Lossing's* The Pictorial Field-Book of the Revolution

CHAPTER I
1492-1664

IN THE BEGINNING

Henry Hudson landed on the shore of New Jersey and claimed it for the Dutch. Photograph courtesy of the New Jersey Historical Society

nly Indians called Lenapes "true men" occupied New Jersey when John Cabot and his son Sebastian, Italian seamen in the service of England, sailed along the New Jersey coast in 1497, claiming the land for England. Giovanni da Verrazano, a Florentine navigator employed by France, is the first known explorer to enter New York Harbor in 1524, establishing France's claim. The Verrazano Bridge between Staten Island and Brooklyn is named for him. Finally Henry Hudson landed at Sandy Hook and proceeded along the coast and up the Hudson River in 1609, claiming the land for Holland.

Dutch settlers, including traders and trappers, occupied Paulus Hook (Jersey City), New Amsterdam (New York City), and Staten Island. A few Dutch trappers and traders followed the famous Indian trails into New Jersey, but no efforts were made to settle beyond the Hudson River. English settlers on the eastern end of Long Island wanted to settle in the area because they wanted full powers of self-government without appeal and no interference in religious matters, but their application was rejected by Peter Stuyvesant, the Dutch governor.

The matter was referred to the directors of Amsterdam, who saw the English as a bulwark against the Indians. They instructed Stuyvesant to negotiate further. The matter became moot when the English attacked the Dutch colony in 1664.

After the Dutch surrendered New Amsterdam to Governor Richard Nichols in 1664, Governor Nichols granted permission to the Long Island men, later known as the Elizabethtown Associates, to settle the hitherto virgin territory along the future Newark Bay and Arthur Kill (Achter-Kull in Dutch).

The men—John Bayly, Daniel Denton, and Luke Watson—all from the eastern end of Long Island, pur-

13

The Half-Moon *was used by Henry Hudson for his successful explorations in 1609. Photograph courtesy of the New Jersey Historical Society*

chased the tract from the Lenape Indians on October 28, 1664. The Indians who signed the deed on Staten Island were Mattano, Sewak-herones, and Warinanco.

The English paid twenty fathoms of trading cloth, two coats, two guns, two kettles, ten bars of lead, twenty handfuls of powder, and 400 fathoms of white wampum. They received more than 35,000 acres of land between the Passaic and Raritan rivers and the Arthur Kill, which extended thirty miles inland. This tract covered portions of what is now Middlesex, Somerset, and Morris counties and all of Essex and Union counties. It appears that the English cheated the Indians. However, since the Indians by tradition owned no land as individuals or groups, it would also appear the Indians drove a hard bargain to obtain articles that they wanted. (Chief Mattano had "sold" the same land to Augustine Hernans, a Dutch agent, in 1651.) Captain John Baker, formerly employed by the Dutch, served as the interpreter in the transaction which took place on Staten Island.

The Elizabethtown Associates were second-generation Americans who had already experienced the difficulties of clearing forests for home sites and gardens and dealing with unfriendly Indians. John Ogden quickly became a leader in the fledgling colony.

In Elizabethtown, with the help of his five sons, other relatives, and neighbors, Ogden quickly felled trees to build the town dam on the creek and the town's first main street. He erected a lumber mill to cut boards for the new houses that were being constructed. Two years later his gristmill and tannery were in operation. He also formed a whaling company in 1669.

Land was divided in Elizabethtown according to shares. Each man received a town lot and a minimum of sixty to seventy acres of land. First lot men, who had the least amount of money invested, received a single tract. Second lot men received double that, and third lot men like Ogden were granted three times that amount.

Like Ogden, who also was a stonemason and bricklayer, the other Associates were craftsmen. Richard Clark was a shipwright; William Hill and William Broadwell, cordwainers; Francis Barber and William Cramer, carpenters; Matthias Hatfield and John Winans, weavers and carpenters.

Meanwhile, back in England, Charles II granted the area taken from the Dutch to his brother James, Duke of York. James, who was in debt, deeded 500,000 acres of the tract to Sir George Carteret and John Lord Berkeley on June 23, 1664. The area included all of what is now Essex and Union counties and portions of Middlesex, Somerset, and Morris counties. The two proprietors outfitted a ship, *The Philip,* to transport Sir George's cousin, Sir Philip Carteret, whom they had appointed governor of their grant. When he arrived at the mouth of the Elizabeth River in August 1665, he was much surprised to see at least four dwellings and to be met by the Associates. The four dwellings and the ship are depicted on the seal of the city of Elizabeth.

Sir Philip Carteret named the new community "Elizabethtown" in honor of Sir George Carteret's wife, Lady Elizabeth. Like the Associates, he began allocating land grants to settlers. As a result there have been title disputes, lawsuits, plots, and torn down fences which have extended into the twentieth century. The Board of Proprietors still maintains offices in Perth Amboy and Burlington to issue deeds to unclaimed land.

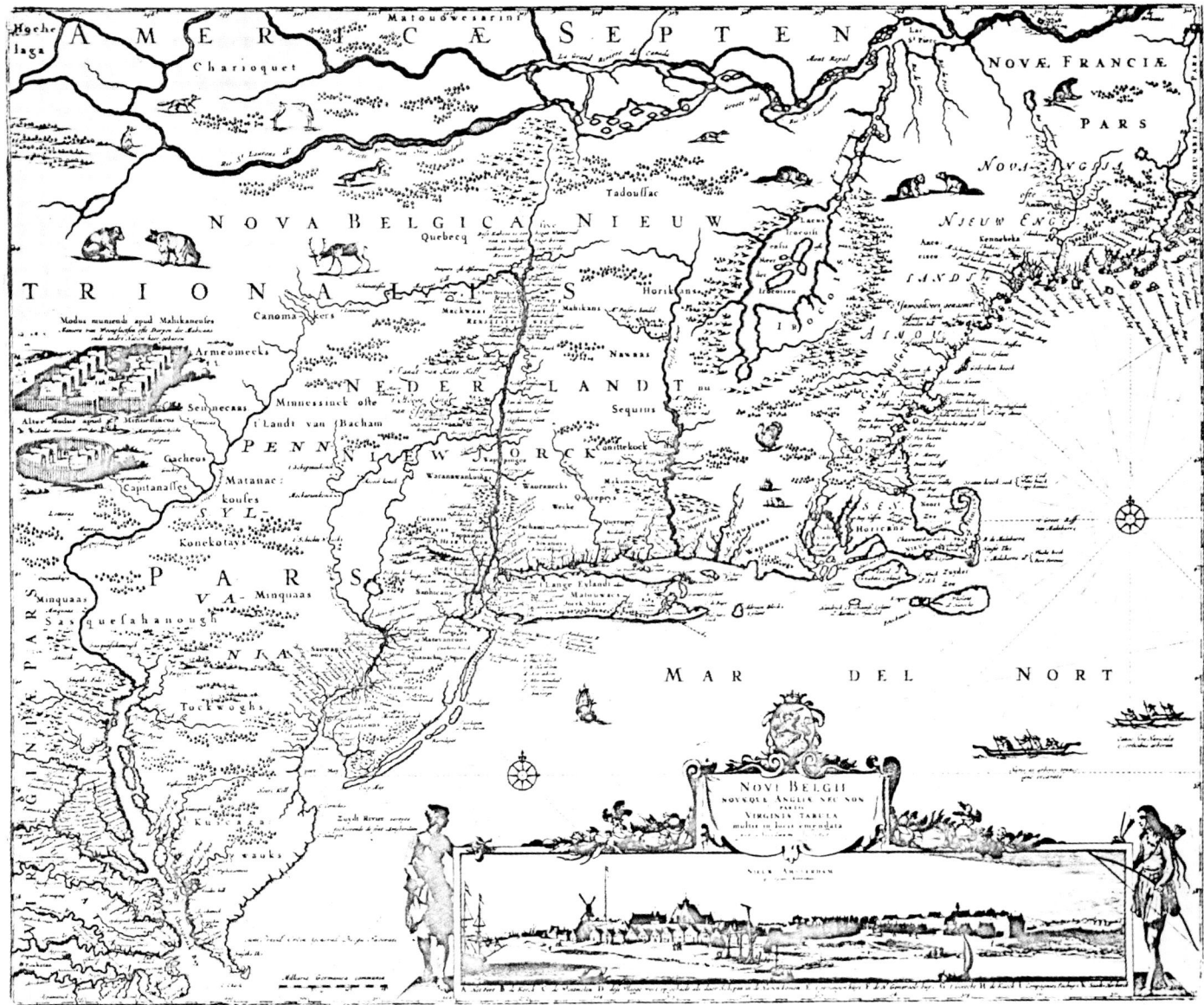

A short time after Carteret's arrival, the inhabitants of Elizabethtown were approached by a Connecticut delegation seeking land. The Elizabethtown peple readily granted them part of the land on the Passaic River. The Newark Town founders arrived in May 1666, landing on a rock in the river. Robert Treat, their leader, is quoted as saying three years later that the "Elizabethtown people were so kind to the Newark people that they couldn't be rewarded enough" (Hatfield, *History of Elizabeth, N. J.*).

The division between the two communities was marked by a chestnut tree on a hill above a swamp near Bound Creek. The site was determined by a prayer, and the hill was named Divident Hill. Essex County was formed in 1683. The first formal line was established by the colony's legislature in 1698.

The grants gave the early settlers town lots, rights to use the meadows for pasture and upland acreage, which they could reach at first only by walking. Soon they were building shelters on them while they farmed the land. In many instances, these areas became known by the farmers' names, such as Woodruff's Farms, Williams' and Lyon's Farms. Williams' Farms became Roselle Park and part of Lyon's Farms became Hillside. Located as it was north of the Elizabethtown hamlet in the partially swampy meadows, Woodruff's Farms could not grow until huge, landmoving equipment created Newark Airport in the twentieth century.

This map by Nicholaus J. Visscher, drawn circa 1656, is called the Novi Belgii map. It was probably used by James, Duke of York, when he decided the boundaries for Nova Caesarea, later New Jersey. Map courtesy of the Alexander Library, Rutgers University

15

David Pierce, John Pike, and Abraham Tappen obtained formal permission on May 21, 1966, from Captain Philip Carteret, who signed the articles of agreement allowing them to settle one or more plantations for townships of from 50 to 100 families. They established Woodbridge Township, but their other settlements extended along the Rahway River and its Robinson's Branch in Rawack, the future Rahway. Communities grew around landings for ships. The Rahway River alone had Shotwell's, Robert Wright's, Bishop's and William Edgar's landings. The last name also was a "corner" (crossroads) on the Woodbridge Road.

In 1683, when counties were formed, the dividing line between Middlesex and Essex counties was the center of the Robinson's Branch of the Rahway River. This division placed part of the Rawack settlement including Bridgetown (so named because it was located at the bridge over the river), Lower Rahway and Leesville in Woodbridge and Middlesex County, and left Spanktown, Rawack, and Milton in Essex County.

All of the early residents, except the thirty colonists and servants brought to the New World by Sir Philip Carteret on *The Philip*, were Puritans or Congregationalists. Carteret's people were either Roman Catholic or Anglicans. All of them were strong monarchists. Thus the seeds for future contention were sown early in the small colony.

Reverend Jonathan Dickinson, who founded the College of New Jersey, the present Princeton University, also was responsible for affiliating his congregation with the Philadelphia Presbyterian Synod. The people who moved inland formed their own Presbyterian churches. The log cabin church at the west fields was founded in the 1730s. the church at the spring fields in 1746 and at Connecticut Farms in 1730. Reverend Mr. Dickinson founded the First Presbyterian Church in Rahway in 1746.

By 1674 there were societies of Friends in Amboy and Woodbridge, and some Quakers from Rawack traveled to those communities for meetings. The first monthly meeting in present-day Union County was established at the home of Joseph Shotwell in Rahway on October 16, 1742. They built their first meetinghouse in 1757 and used it until 1804, when it was taken over by the First Methodist

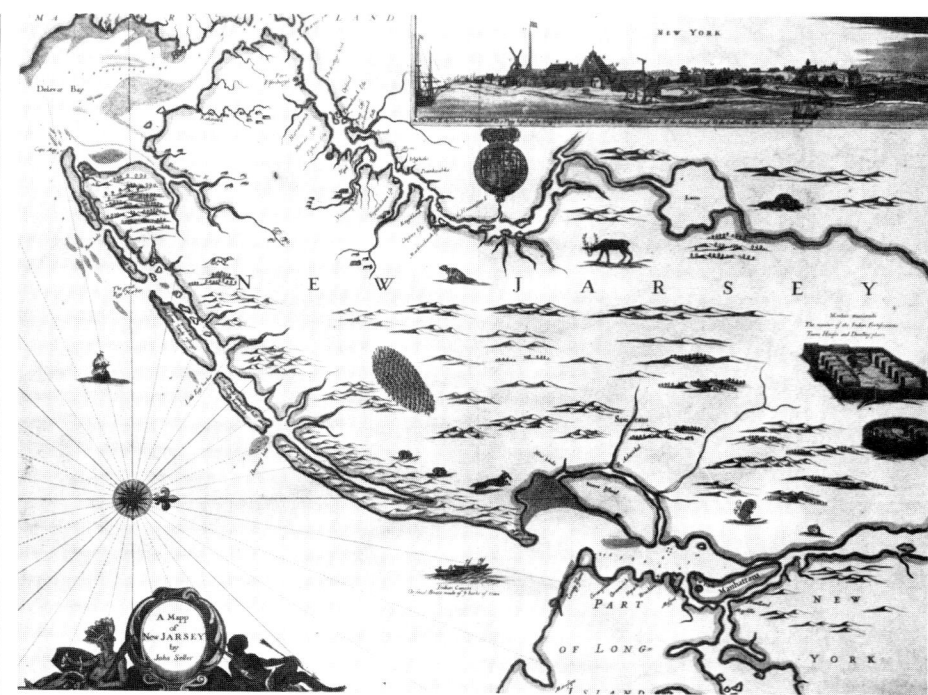

The earliest map of the "New Jarsey" area was made by John Sellers. It shows New Jersey from New York and places New Jersey on top of New York. Map courtesy of the New Jersey Historical Society

Captain Philip Carteret landed at the new English settlement in August 1665. He was sent to the New World by his cousin and patron, Sir George Carteret of the Isle of Jersey. Sir George and Lord John Berkeley were deeded the area by James, Duke of York, in payment of debts. Captain Carteret named the new community Elizabethtown in honor of Sir George Carteret's wife and the new colony New Jersey in honor of Sir George Carteret's home of Jersey. This painting hangs in the Hall of Records, Newark. Photograph courtesy of the Newark Public Library

Society. The Quakers were operating a schoolhouse by 1785.

Meanwhile more Quakers were moving into Mill Town, New Brooklyn, Samptown, or Tow Town, as a portion of the plain fields was called by 1728, and settling along Green Brook. At one time there were two meetings in the area. The present building was erected in 1788.

Shortly after the turn of the century a third religious group, the Baptists, began to move up the Raritan River and settle in Piscataway. By 1707 they had formed a congregation. Some of these moved into the Scot's Plains area where the Scotch Plains Baptist Church was organized on September 8, 1747. The Baptists continued to move northeast until the Lyon's Farms Baptist Church was organized on April 16, 1769. ■

Left: This is an artist's depiction of the purchase of Elizabethtown from the Indians on October 28, 1664. Photograph courtesy of the Elizabeth Public Library

Lady Elizabeth Carteret for whom Elizabethtown was named. Her cousin, Governor Philip Carteret later married Elizabeth Smith Lawrence, a widow, who also was called Lady Elizabeth Carteret. After Carteret's death, the American Lady Carteret married Richard Townley and founded a long line of descendants. This painting hangs in the Elizabeth Public Library. Photograph by Richard T. Koles

Divident Hill is the traditional boundary line between Elizabethtown and Newark Town. Representatives of Elizabethtown and Newark Town met on the hill in May 1668 to determine the boundary. The boundary was moved nearly a half-mile south when Union County was formed in 1857. The monument was built in 1916, when the area became Weequahic Park, Newark. Photograph by Richard T. Koles

The Hetfield house stood on Pearl Street near the Elizabethtown Creek (the Elizabeth River), Elizabethtown. It is believed to have been built in 1667. According to tradition, early Indian treaties were made between the settlers and the people in this house. It was burned in 1927, in 1942, and in 1943, when it was razed. Photograph courtesy of the Elizabeth Public Library

The Nathaniel Bonnel house at 1045 East Jersey Street, Elizabeth, was built prior to 1682. It currently houses the headquarters of the New Jersey Society, Sons of the American Revolution, and the Elizabethtown Chapter No. 1, SAR. It is believed to be the oldest house still standing in Elizabeth. Chapter No. 1 was organized on September 26, 1893, as an outgrowth of a patriotic celebration July 4, 1893, at the First Presbyterian Church. The chapter collects and preserves relics and records, celebrates anniversaries, marks historic sites, cares for graves of Revolutionary War veterans, and erects tablets and monuments at historic sites. It is open on Tuesdays and Thursdays. Photograph by Richard T. Koles

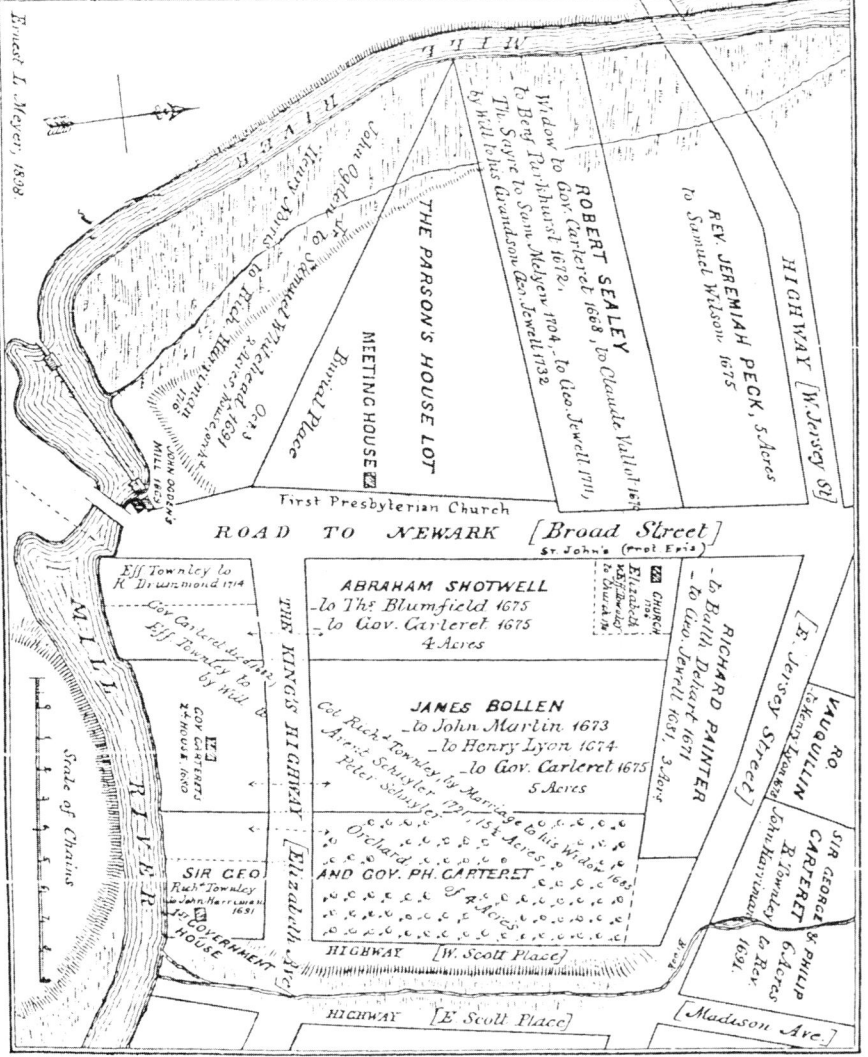

This Ernest L. Meyer map, drawn in 1898, shows early land holdings in Elizabethtown. Mill River was also known as the Elizabeth Creek or the Elizabeth River. Photograph courtesy of the Elizabeth Public Library

William Robinson, a doctor of medicine, purchased 700 acres on Robinson's Branch of the Rahway River about 1690, built this English Tudor-style dwelling, and practiced medicine. Queen Elizabeth I of England would have been right at home if she had visited the house in Rahway. It has many architectural features which were popular in her day, including casement windows and the overhanging second story, which can be seen at the left of the building. After Rahway became a city, the area around the plantation was designated as the Fifth Ward. The Fifth Ward became Clark Township in 1864. The Clark Historical Society has preserved the house. Photograph by Richard T. Koles

Reverend Jonathan Dickinson, pastor of the Presbyterian church in Elizabethtown, was a busy man. He served from 1709 until his death in 1747. While pastor, he started the churches in Westfield, Connecticut Farms, Rahway, and New Providence and served as first president of the College of New Jersey (now Princeton). He also wrote extensively. Photograph of painting in the Princeton University Library

When British raiders were anticipated in the West Fields, the people in the village carried their valuables to the old Badgley farmhouse on the New Providence Road (now in Mountainside) for safekeeping. The raiders climbed the hills to the house and ransacked it. They carried away "quantities of linen, clothing, silver, a number of silk gowns owned by a lady in West Fields and a state lottery ticket" (Anniversary Program). The house, built in 1738, was used by farmers for barn dances, barn raisings, and barbecues. Located in the Watchung Reservation, it has been used for storage by the county's parks. The hill behind the house was called Pot Luck. Photograph from the Official Program 200th Anniversary of the Settlement of Westfield, 1720-1920; courtesy of the Westfield Historical Society

The French family was one of the first to move into the west fields area. Their house stood on Clark Place, Westfield. Photograph courtesy of the Westfield Historical Society

Peter Wilcox (also spelled Willcock, Willcocks, or Willcoxsie) and his brother-in-law, Joseph Badgley, acquired the valley between First and Second mountains behind the west fields in 1720 and settled it in 1736. They operated grist and sawmills on Blue Brook, a tributary of Green Brook, and mined copper. The area became known as Peter's Hill and the spring as Indian Spring because Indians are believed to have used the valley as a winter campsite. The mill was used to make gunpowder during the Revolutionary War and the War of 1812. This is the tombstone of John Willcocks. Photograph courtesy of the Newark Public Library

The Old Fort on Thompson's Lane near Bridge Street, Elizabethtown, was built in 1734. It was used as a home by Cortlandt Van Ansdol and William Shute. The building was demolished in 1932. Photograph from Elizabeth Board of Trade Souvenir Program, 1907

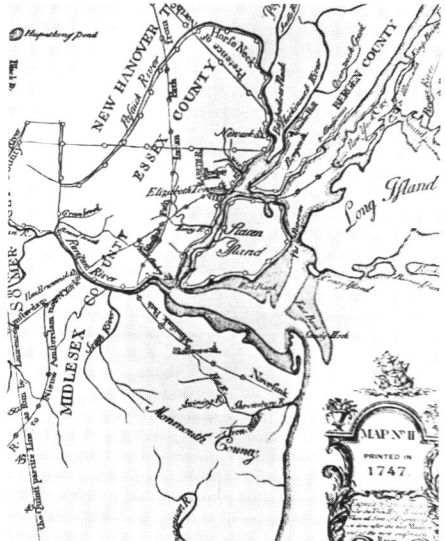

This map, engraved in 1747 by James Turner, is believed to be the earliest map of the Elizabethtown area. Map courtesy of Arthur F. Cole

The Sayre house on Sayre Lake in Summit was built in the early part of the eighteenth century from stone found in the woods nearby. There is a legend that George Washington stopped by the front door to ask for a drink of water in June 1780. The house was in the Sayre family until 1954. It was used as an antique shop, music studio, and gallery for African art. Now owned by former Deputy Attorney General William and Mrs. Eleanor Gural, it is a private residence. Photograph by Richard T. Koles

Connecticut Farms was settled by a group of farmers from Connecticut in 1667. Many of them were related to the settlers in both Newark Town and Elizabethtown. The church was the center of the small community. Colonel Elias Dayton faced the British near the church during the Battle of Connecticut Farms. The church and several houses were burned during the British retreat from the Battle at the Spring Fields on June 23, 1780. This church was constructed after the war. Photograph (circa 1900) from Charles Aquilina's collection

The First Presbyterian Church, Elizabeth, circa 1967. Photograph by Donald Davidson

Death was a frequent visitor for people in Elizabethtown. The gravestones for two brothers, among the oldest in the First Presbyterian Church graveyard, are in the foundation of the church. Both died in 1687. Photograph by Donald Davidson

This photograph of St. John's Church, Elizabeth, was made from an old lithograph. George Keith, representing the Society for the Propagation of the Gospel in Foreign Parts, started the Anglican church in 1703. Reverend Edward Vaughn served as the church's rector for thirty-eight years, the same term Reverend Jonathan Dickinson, the Presbyterian minister, served. They died the same week. Photograph courtesy of the Elizabeth Public Library

CHAPTER II
1664-1775

OUT OF THE WILDERNESS... ELIZABETHTOWN

Reverend Thomas Bradbury Chandler, rector of St. John's Church, Elizabethtown, succeeded Vaughn. He supported the Crown throughout the Revolutionary War period, fleeing to England for the duration. He returned to Elizabethtown in 1785 and was permitted to resume his pulpit. Photograph courtesy of St. John's Church

The old St. John's parsonage was built about 1688 by Andrew Hamton. It was deeded to the wardens and vestrymen of St. John's Church on December 1749 by Captain John Emmott and his wife for £162 New Jersey money. It was occupied by rectors of St. John's Church, from Reverend Thomas B. Chandler, D.D. (1748-1790) to Reverend Samuel A. Clark, D.D. (1856-1875). Reverend Mr. Chandler's wife was Jane Emmott, daughter of Captain John Emmott, a brother-in-law of Elias Boudinot. The parsonage was enlarged in 1765 and in 1817-18. It also was used as a school by three rectors in the 1800s. It became a missionary house in 1885, and it was used as a convalescent and mission house until 1902, when it was sold to Pasquale Girolamo. Carmelo Tavormina, his wife, and Rose Genova became the owners in 1919. By 1940 Rose Genova was the sole owner. It is now preserved by the Elizabethtown Historical Foundation. Photograph courtesy of the Elizabeth Public Library

hurch and God, law and order and hardwork were the keystones to the new settlers' lives. Despite the 3,000-mile distance between the new colony and the motherland, English customs and frailties prevailed.

His Royal Highness, James, Duke, of York, concurred with the Long Islanders without knowing it when he directed that the new land be purchased from the Indian *sachems* ("chiefs") and recorded by the royal governor. All lands would remain with their purchasers and their heirs as free lands to be disposed of as they pleased.

"Liberty of conscience" was guaranteed provided "such liberty is not converted to licentiousness or the disturbance of others in the exercise of the Protestant religion" (Hatfield, *History of Elizabeth, N.J.*). The towns also were given the right to make laws, elect both civic and military officers, and decide all small causes among themselves. In exchange they were required to take an oath of allegiance to the king and pay required sums to the minister.

Governor Philip Carteret, who is said to have shouldered a hoe to be as one with the Long Islanders, granted the settlers the Concessions and Agreements, considered to be a major advance in self-government. Each township was free to elect its own officers, magistrates, fenceviewers, and other officials and to provide its own civil and military protection. The governor named a council of six to twelve people to assist him. A secretary or register recorded all public affairs, and a surveyor-general surveyed, certified, and registered the lands. The residents selected twelve representatives who met annually with the governor and council to make laws. The assembly also appointed as many ministers or preachers as necessary.

25

The Merchants' and Drovers' Tavern, Rahway, located on St. George's Avenue, the old King's Highway, has had many names, including the Rahway Hotel, Roberts' Hotel, the Farmers' and Mechanics', Swindlinger's Hotel, Lambert's Hotel, and St. George Hotel. It was one of several inns along the highway. Built in 1750, it was used as an inn until 1932, then as the Rahway area Girl Scout house until the Rahway Historical Society began restoring it. Circa 1920. Photograph courtesy of the Rahway Historical Society

Most of the General Assemblies were held in Elizabethtown, where Carteret lived, on the first Tuesday in November. Because of this, ELizabethtown is considered the first capital of New Jersey. Other assemblies were held in Woodbridge, Middletown, and Piscataway. When Jonathan Belcher became governor, he moved the capital, then located in Burlington, back to Elizabethtown. He moved into the dwelling now known as the Belcher-Ogden mansion.

The assembly was busy and justice was swift. Men between sixteen and sixty were required to provide themselves with arms to protect the settlements against hostile Indians, the Dutch, or other enemies. Burglars and highway robbers had their hands burned for the first offense, their foreheads burned for the second and third offenses, and they were put to death for additional misdemeanors. Persons who conspired to attack towns and forts were also punished by death. Undutiful children who struck or cursed their parents could be punished by death, except when they were provoked. In the case of adultery or fornication, the party was to be divorced, forced to marry, or submit to corporal punishment, fined or banished. For nightwalking and reveling after 9 p.m., the guilty parties would be secured by the constable, the community's first law enforcement officer, until morning and held until the next court day if answers were unsatisfactory. Consent of parents, masters, or overseers had to be given for each marriage. The bans had to be published three times in some public meeting or kirk (church), or put in writing at the public house or inn. Each community was required to have at least one inn or tavern. Prices for lodging, meats, liquor, and care of horses were fixed by law.

Both the Associates and the Proprietors encouraged settlements. The colony grew unevenly. Peter Wilcox and his brother-in-law Joseph Badgley settled in the valley between First and Second Mountains near Indian Springs, reportedly a favorite camp site of the Lenape Indians. The men built a dam across Blue Brook and operated grist and saw mills. They also mined copper. The area became known as Peter's Hill.

This ancient marker once stood on the King's Highway, now St. George's Avenue. Courtesy of the Newark Public Library

The Williams homestead was one of the earliest dwellings in Williams' Farms (now Roselle Park). It was located on the Westfield Road (now Westfield Avenue) between Chestnut and Walnut streets. The house was moved back when the road was straightened about 1900. Still standing, the house is now joined to commercial buildings. Photograph courtesy of the Roselle Park Historical Society

The mills were used to make gunpowder during the Revolutionary War and the War of 1812.

Some settled in Turkey, so called because of the abundance of wild game. It is said that after a balcony fell without injuring anyone during a service in the church, the congregation dubbed the section "New Providence" because all were spared.

Church attendance was both a duty and a social function. Distances from the outlying farms made it an all-day event. Picnic lunches were eaten on the lawns in good weather. The people walked to church and home again because of the absence of roads and horses.

Early millers sought sites along the Elizabeth, Rahway and Passaic rivers, Morss's Creek, Green and Cedar brooks, where the waters might be dammed, meadows flooded, and mill races built for early saw, grain, and paper mills. Members of the Crane family built both on the Elizabeth River at Crane's Mills, Elizabethtown, and at Crane's Mills or Crane's Ford (Cranford). William Bradford, the first printer in the American colonies, built a paper mill probably on the East Branch of the Elizabeth River. John Marsh received permission in 1683 to construct a sawmill and in 1684 a gristmill on the Rahway River. William Looker, a brewer, received a license from the Proprietors of East Jersey in 1686 to stop the South Branch of the Elizabeth River "to drown a certain quantity of meadow to erect a mill" (Clayton, *History of Union and Middlesex Counties, N. J.*). Jonathan Bishop was granted permission to build a gristmill on the South Branch of the same river, then called Mill Brook. There was a Mill Town in both the plain fields and the spring fields.

Roads were cut across fields and through the woods to connect the Stone Bridge in Elizabethtown with Newark Town, the center of the hamlet with the Arthur Kill, Elizabethtown with Rawack, the hamlets with the mills. They were called the King's Highway, the Road to Williams' Farms, the Upper and Lower roads to Newark, the Road to Jewell's Mill or the Road to Rahway.

As the community grew, the houses grew. In some instances, the householders tore down the original shanties to build newer and larger houses. In most instances, they added two-and-a-half-story sections to the original one-story dwellings. Craftsmen frequently added small workshops or shops in which to make and sell their wares. They included William Letts, a weaver; Robert Wright, a tanner; and Henry Jaques, Sr., a carpenter, all of Rawack; Richard Painter, tailor; James and John Hinds, coopers; Aaron Miller, a clockmaster; Isaac Whitehead, a shoemaker, all of Elizabethtown; John Magie of Magietown (now part of Elizabeth), a blacksmith; Benjamin Wade of Wade's Farms (Union Township), a clothier; and Leonard Headley of Headleytown (Union Township), maker of barrel staves for liquor and molasses barrels.

Some of the new houses were built of stone and brick. Andrew Hampton, a tailor, eloped with "Lady" Margaret Cummins and in 1697 built the dwelling near the Elizabeth River which later became the St. John's Parsonage.

From the start, chickens, cattle, and sheep were confined behind fences,

The Isaac Drake house was built on the Old York Road in 1746 in the plain fields below the Blue Hills. The dwelling was used by General George Washington during the Battle of the Short Hills on June 26, 1777. One hundred twenty years later, it was sold to Joseph Harberger, a wealthy businessman, who enlarged and Victorianized it. It was sold by his estate on April 26, 1917, to Mr. and Mrs. Siegmund Frucht. Police raided the house during World War I and found a great deal of seditious literature. The house was unoccupied for a year or so. In the early 1920s Bertram F. Tallamy purchased it and conveyed it to the West End Civic Association of Plainfield on the same day. Title was transferred also on the same day to the Historical Society of Plainfield and North Plainfield. It now is owned by the city of Plainfield, which maintains it as a historical museum. Photograph by Richard T. Koles

This ancient fireplace in the Drake house has been restored to its pre-Revolutionary appearance. Photograph by Richard T. Koles

both to keep them out of gardens and to keep them safe from Indians. The Indians are described by Samuel Smith in *The History of the Colony of Nova-Caesaria or New Jersey* as being "in person upright and straight in their limbs. Their bodies were strong, but of a strength rather fitted to endure hardships than to sustain much bodily labour. They were seldom crooked or deformed. Their features were regular .... Their behavior in publick councils was strictly decent and instructive. Everyone in his turn was heard according to rank or years or wisdom of services to his country. Not a word or a whisper or a murmur [was made] while any spoke. [There was]...no interruption to commend or condemn. The younger sort were totally silent."

The Indians caused minor disturbances but usually were friendly. Some of them were enslaved, as were blacks who began arriving in the colony early in the eighteenth century. Most of the principal families owned them, but slavery was never as economically feasible in New Jersey as it was in the

The Presbyterian Church, Westfield, as seen from the Revolutionary War Cemetery, where fifty-one veterans are buried. Photograph by Richard T. Koles

Peter Kean, then a child, greets Lenape Indians in Elizabethtown in 1796. By this time, the Indians were becoming scarce. The first Indian reservation was established at Brotherton in 1758. It later was renamed Indian Mills. The experiment was unsuccessful, and in 1801, when only about 100 Indians were left, the group voted to join their relatives in New Stockbridge, Lake Oneida, New York. This group moved to Green Bay, Wisconsin, in 1822. Some of the Lenapes may be found on reservations in Oklahoma, where these Indians joined the Cherokee Nation, and in Ontario, Canada. This is a photograph of a painting in the Union County Courthouse Annex, Elizabeth. Photograph courtesy of Arthur F. Cole

South.

Many of the early residents were bond servants. Recruited in Europe, their boat passage was paid by either the ship companies or people in the colonies who wanted servants. When they completed paying for their passage, usually by seven years of hard work, they were given land. A few of Carteret's party also were paid servants who were allotted land.

The honeymoon with Governor Carteret ended when the Elizabethans objected to paying quitrents—paid by freemen in lieu of services required of them by feudal custom. None was charged during the first five years of the Elizabethtown Colony from 1665, when Carteret arrived. They were due in 1670. The Associates, who considered themselves freemen, refused to pay them, claiming that under the Nichols patent none was due. The protest against taxes to the British crown would continue until the adoption of the Stamp Act some 100 years later hurled the colonies into the Revolution.

As always, there were poor members of the community. The lowest bidder at a public auction would provide board and lodging to those unable to care for themselves. Both were guaranteed to be meager. In time a combined poorhouse, workhouse, and house of correction was built.

As the colony grew older, richer people moved into it. One of these, William Livingston, a New York lawyer, built his mansion on the outskirts of Elizabethtown and eventually retired there. Elias Boudinot, also a lawyer, moved to the center of town.

Stagecoaches began to appear on the roads along with farm wagons and to make regular trips between New York and Philadelphia through Elizabethtown. The town had long been a ferry point to New York.

Most of the early residents could read, write, and calculate a little. Women, usually widows, conducted "dame schools" at their homes to teach the children so that they could at least read their Bibles. A requisite for the early ministers was that they teach the students.

The Lyon's Farms School was started by the farmers in 1728, and the Academy was organized in 1766 in Elizabethtown.

Religion continued to be the center of most people's social life. In the 1740s, the Great Religious Awakening swept the colonies. George Whitefield was among the evangelists who visited Elizabethtown.

The New Jersey Brigade, the famous "Jersey Blues," was raised by 1756 to go to the New York Colony in the French and Indian War. Among the troops was young Captain Elias Dayton, then only nineteen years old.

By the time Elizabethtown celebrated its 100th anniversary on October 28, 1764, it was a prosperous farm area. Some fifty variety of apples alone were grown in Lyon's Farms; cider mills made the famous Jersey Lightning; Jonathan Hampton was making fine coaches; Benjamin and Matthias Halsted were making silver articles; and Elizabethtown merchants were engaged in an active coastwise and Caribbean trade. ■

This is the Caldwell parsonage, site of the murder of Hannah Ogden Caldwell, wife of Reverend James Caldwell, the fighting parson. He was so named because of the caustic sermons he preached at the First Presbyterian Church of Elizabethtown and because he was both chaplain and head of ordnance with the Third New Jersey Regiment.

The British hated him because of his strong opposition to them. It was felt that his wife's death was caused by them because of their feelings for him. After the murder the original house was burned. This dwelling was built after the war. It was spared from destruction in 1958 by the formation of the Union Township Historical Society. It is maintained as a museum. Both the parsonage, once used by the pastors of the Connecticut Farms Presbyterian Church, Union Township, and the street on which it stands are named for the Caldwells. Photograph by Richard T. Koles

Left: The home of Frederick S. Best, president of the Berkeley Heights Historical Society, and Mrs. Lois Best was built in 1740 by Nathaniel Smith. The Bests purchased and restored the house in 1945. Photograph by Charles L. Aquilina

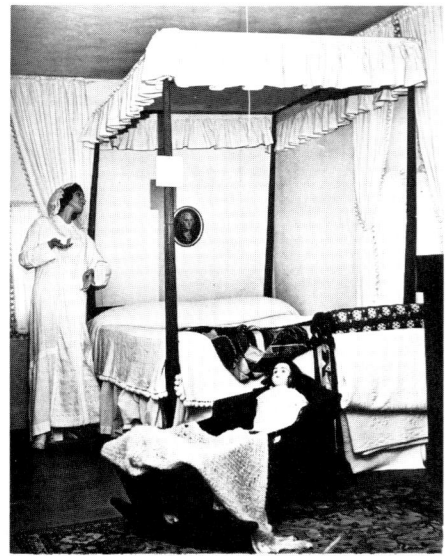

Bedroom in Caldwell parsonage, Union Township, contains canopied bed, baby's cradle, and blanket rack. Photograph by Richard T. Koles

Ye Olde Meeker Inn was built in 1756 by Joseph Meeker in Connecticut Farms, now Union Township. It was operated by the Meekers throughout the nineteenth century. The building was removed in the 1920s for the construction of the Union Center National Bank building. According to local tradition, the inn escaped the torch in 1780 because no road passed before its door. The Morris Turnpike was built in 1804. Photograph courtesy of the Newark Public Library

Royal Governor Jonathan Belcher of New Jersey previously served as governor of Massachusetts. His library forms the nucleus of the Firestone Library at Princeton University. New Jersey State Governor Aaron Ogden also resided in the house now known as the Belcher-Ogden mansion. It was preserved by the Elizabethtown Historical Foundation, when its removal was desired to enlarge the parking lot of the Elizabeth Police Station. All ornaments and furnishings in the mansion belong to the Revolutionary War period. Photograph of a painting in the Belcher-Ogden mansion by Richard T. Koles

Delft tiles were imported from Holland to decorate the fireplace in the Belcher-Ogden mansion. Photograph by Richard T. Koles

This china candleholder in the Belcher-Ogden mansion, Elizabeth, is said to have been used at the wedding of Catherine Smith to Elisha Boudinot. Photograph by Richard T. Koles

Reverend Jonathan Edwards visited Governor Jonathan Belcher at the Belcher-Ogden mansion on several occasions. A tiny closet-like room on the second floor of the mansion was used by him as a library. His daughter married Aaron Burr, Sr., and became the mother of Aaron Burr, Jr. Many of Edwards' descendants still reside in Union County. From a painting by C. W. Peale, engraved by J. D. Gross, printed by J. M. Butler; photograph by Richard T. Koles

The Boudinot mansion was known as Boxwood Hall. Elias Boudinot entertained President-elect George Washington at luncheon on April 23, 1789. Boudinot served as president of the Continental Congress. The hall was used as the Home for Aged Women before it was purchased and restored by the state of New Jersey. Photograph by Richard T. Koles

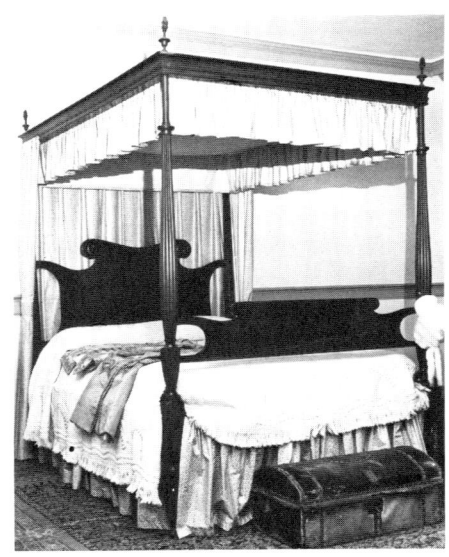

A bedroom in Boxwood Hall. The murdered body of Reverend James Caldwell was carried to the front steps of this mansion after he was killed at the ferry. Photograph by Richard T. Koles

Dining room in Boxwood Hall. Jonathan Dayton, the signer of the Declaration of Independence, entertained Marquise de Lafayette in the hall of 1824. Photograph by Richard T. Koles

Elias Boudinot, president of the Continental Congress and the American Bible Society, was Washington's right-hand man in the Revolutionary War. Photograph courtesy of the Newark Public Library

Mrs. Elias Boudinot, IV, the former Hannah Stockton of Princeton. From a painting by C. W. Peale at Princeton University; photograph by Richard T. Koles

Revolutionary cannon stood ready for action in Union Township. Photograph (circa 1910) courtesy of the Union Township Police Department

Royal Governor William Franklin was New Jersey's last royal governor, serving from 1762 to 1776. From painting in the Philadelphia Public Library; photograph by Richard T. Koles

Abraham Clark of Wheatsheaf (now Roselle), was the only signer of the Declaration of Independence from north of the Raritan River in New Jersey. He was known as the "poor man's lawyer" because he never asked fees from those who could not afford them. He pushed a law through the state legislature known as Clark's laws, which restricted the power of lawyers and lessened court costs. From the painting in the State House, Trenton; photograph courtesy of Newark Public Library

CHAPTER III
1775-1800

ELIZABETHTOWN— GATEWAY TO THE REVOLUTION

The recreated Abraham Clark house, Roselle. Photograph by Richard T. Koles

Grave of Abraham Clark in Rahway Cemetery. Photograph by Richard T. Koles

Theodore Thayer called the area that now comprises Union County the Gateway to New Jersey. Elizabethtown's crucial defensive position was recognized by the British when the barracks were established in 1754.

"Elizabethtown was an important town on one of the main roads from New York to Philadelphia. The British kept a company of troops barracked there until 1774. Though the citizens did not object—the soldiers were good spenders—patriotic influence did take root there, in stark contrast with neighboring Staten Island. Of New Jersey's five delegates to the First Continental Congress, three (Stephen Crane, William Livingston and John De Hart) were of Elizabethtown" *Staten Island Historian,* vol. xxxii March, 1973.

Prior to war, a number of acts indicated the hostility of the area against the British. William Peartree Smith, chairman of the Committee of Correspondence of New Jersey, wrote to a similar committee in Boston, "The arbitrary and cruel oppression under which your Metropolis now labors from the suspension of commerce, must inevitably reduce multitudes to inexpressible difficulty and distress." His letter also promised much-needed help which, of course, was accepted.

Elias Boudinot, chairman of a secret committee, sent gunpowder to General George Washington. In all, about ten tons were secreted in "rackriggins covered with hay to allay suspicion." General Washington thanked "the committee from the Southern region" (Hatfield, *History of Elizabeth, N. J.*).

The martial spirit of Elizabethtown was demonstrated on October 4, 1775,

35

This map shows the routes taken in the capture of the Blue Mountain Valley *on January 22, 1776. Map from Charles L. Aquilina's* The Capture of His Majesty's Blue Mountain Valley

when the newly-organized sixteen companies of infantry and militia were reviewed on the parade grounds near the Presbyterian church by family-folk and friends. The most eye-catching was the company of Plumed Light Horse commanded by Colonel Mathias Williamson.

In November, Congress established a recruiting station in Elizabethtown, and Colonel William Alexander, Earl of Stirling, organized the First New Jersey Regiment of Volunteers. Violence and bloodshed were still far away.

Only two months later the most serious organized military action by a New Jersey group before the signing of the Declaration of Independence was taken. Between 11 a.m. and 12 noon on January 22, 1776, Colonel Alexander with about forty men set out for Amboy on an "important enterprise" to capture the *Blue Mountain Valley,* a British cargo ship anchored off Staten Island in Princess (or Prince's) Bay.

In the afternoon, an express rider arrived in Elizabethtown with a letter directed to Colonel Alexander or, in his absence, the chairman of the local committee. The dispatch stated that an armed vessel with a detachment of marines and seamen was on its way from New York Harbor. Chairman Robert Ogden called the Elizabethtown committee and advised the members of the "serious enterprise" (Hatfield, *History of Elizabeth, N. J.*) and the potential danger of Colonel ALexander and his men.

The committee quickly organized volunteers to be led by Colonel Elias Dayton and Lieutenant Colonel Edward Thomas to sail to Amboy to warn and assist Colonel Alexander. Three or four boats were outfitted. Between midnight and 1 a.m. about eighty volunteers sailed toward the narrows. They were forced to turn back because the ice and tide were too formidable. They decided instead to go along the Arthur Kill.

With luck and a fair wind, they arrived in Amboy just before dawn and met Colonel Alexander and his men. They joined forces and sailed into the sunrise, sighting and boarding the *Blue Mountain Valley* without incident.

The prize, enroute to Boston from England, was brought to Elizabethtown several days later. The cargo of coal, hogs, beans, and potatoes was sold at public auction. Colonel Alexander reserved a portion of the coal for Moses Ogden, Sr., who was doing iron work for the military.

The successful, though hurried venture, was to prove an omen for the course of the war in New Jersey. By year's end, Elizabethans were celebrating General Washington's stunning victory at Trenton, considered a turning point in the war. Both events displayed the daring and resolve of the commitment to freedom. The next six years would truly test the strength and staying power of that commitment.

Colonel Alexander with four companies was ordered to New York City on February 5. General Livingston, his brother-in-law, had ordered 300 militiamen to the eastern end of Long Island to defend it when word was received that Sir Henry Clinton had sailed from Boston with some 10,000 troops. Considering the size of Sir Henry's forces, the local action almost bordered on rashness.

In mid-March, earthworks were thrown up along the waterfront opposite Staten Island, only 600 feet away. As more British sails were sighted along the coast, apprehension grew. The proximity of the British navy prompted Abraham Clark to write, "If all the congresses upon the continent required of us to disarm ourselves at present...I would not obey" (Hatfield, *History of Elizabeth, N. J.*).

More earthworks were constructed by late March under the supervision of General William Thompson. Colonel Elias Dayton was ordered to march the Third Battalion to the defense of New York City. General Livingston wrote to General Washington on July 4, "Thrown up a couple of small breast works over the salt meadows. We have two field-pieces with a part of a company of artillery [Captain Daniel Neill's] of the

The Minute Man Statue in Elizabeth stands at the Crossroads, where Moses Ogden, then nineteen years old, accompanied by eleven other Continental soldiers faced 6,000 British and Hessian soldiers. The small force fired. One of the bullets struck General Thomas Stirling, the British commander. He died shortly afterward.

Young Ogden died later the same day at Connecticut Farms. The Crossroads mark the dividing spot between Elizabeth and "the Port." Photograph by Richard T. Koles.

The Scotch Plains Baptist parsonage, built in 1786, apparently replaced an earlier one that burned. Photograph (1875) by Guillermo Thorn

Aaron Burr, Jr. Photograph courtesy of the Newark Public Library

Aaron Burr's dueling pistols and Peter Stuyvesant's tinderbox were stolen from the Van Cortlandt Museum on November 9, 1976, and recovered by New Jersey State Police on the New Jersey Turnpike by November 22, 1976. It is believed that the pistols were used in the fatal duel with Alexander Hamilton. Photograph courtesy of New Jersey Newsphotos, Inc.

Province."

"The two field-pieces very soon gave a good account of themselves," according to Edwin F. Hatfield in his *History of Elizabeth in Union County.* "One of the enemy's armed sloops of fourteen guns...ran near Elizabethtown Point at midnight July 4, 1776, and was attacked from the shore with [the] two twelve-pounders. A great number of her men were killed. She was set on fire and entirely destroyed."

This attack by Captain Neill, which coincided with the official date for the signing of the Declaration of Independence by Abraham Clark of Elizabethtown, is considered to be the first action in the war.

General Livingston, a resident of what is now Union County, resigned his command when he was selected New Jersey's first governor on August 31, 1776. The command of the New Jersey Militia was transferred to Colonel Mathias Williamson, who was commissioned a brigadier general.

The defeat of Long Island on August 27, 1776, forced the retreat of Washington's army across Manhattan Island to White Plains. General Washington placed New Jersey on alert on November 7, 1776. He directed Governor Livingston that all livestock, food stuff, and anything of value to the enemy be removed. He concluded, "Not a blade of grass should remain for their use" (Hatfield, *History of Elizabeth, N. J.*).

General Mathias Williamson, on hearing of the capture of Forts Washington on Manhattan Island and Lee on the Jersey-side of the Hudson River, wrote to Colonel Jacob Ford at Morristown, "You are ordered to bring out the militia...and march them to Elizabethtown...with four days provisions."

General Washington meanwhile retreated to the almost deserted Newark Town, leaving most of his supplies behind him. He stayed in Newark six days before resuming the march south. "His army left one end of the town, as the British came in the other," one observer wrote. During this time Thomas Paine penned the words, "These are the times that try men's souls."

As Washington's tattered army of about 3,500 troops marched through Elizabethtown, the cause for liberty looked hopeless. These were the darkest days of the conflict. Ashbel Green wrote, "The whole population could have been bought for eighteen pence a

Alexander Hamilton. Etching courtesy of the Newark Public Library

Aaron Burr, Jr., as an old man. From a painting by Oliver I. Lay at the Century Club, New York City; photograph courtesy of the Alexander Library, Rutgers University

William Alexander, Lord Stirling, a brother-in-law of New Jersey's first state governor, William Livingston, was placed in charge of the Elizabethtown troops. Before the war ended, he commanded every brigade except those in South Carolina and Georgia. Photograph from Benson J. Lossing's The Pictorial Field-Book of the Revolution

head." General Lord William Howe announced on arrival in Elizabethtown that he would publish "pardon and peace" to all inhabitants who desired it. He gave sixty days of grace.

About 6,000 British and Hessian troops occupied Elizabethtown in December. Foraging parties scoured Elizabethtown for hay and grain and transported it to New York City. During these dark days, there were several signs of continued spunk among the rebels. A group of discouraged townsmen met at Isaac Arnett's home to discuss the British offer of amnesty. Arnett's wife, Hannah, listened in an adjoining room. Suddenly she entered the room and told the assembled men that she would be ashamed of anyone who gave up. "That would be a traitor's choice," she declared. The men reconsidered.

Another bright incident is the little-known first Battle of Springfield on December 17, 1776. General Lord Charles Cornwallis sent out a company of 1,500 men from the Waldeckers, a mercenary unit, and General Leslie's brigade to Elizabethtown to drive off the militia threatening his rear flank from their stronghold at the Short Hills behind the spring fields.

Major Oliver Spencer, who occupied the spring fields, withdrew toward Chatham. Captain Job Brookfield attacked the right flank on the Vauxhall Road, and Captain Sylvanus Seeley attacked the left on the West Fields Road. The conflict lasted an hour, ceasing because of darkness. The Continentals

This is a copy of an original sketch made by William Alexander, Lord Stirling, for a log beacon atop First Mountain. Sentries lighted it to alert the countryside when British troop movements or invasions were observed from New York City or Staten Island. One of these was at the Gap in the Short Hills behind the spring fields. This was renamed Hobart's Gap. Another beacon was on Tin Kettle Hill (in Kenilworth) above Crane's Ford, and a third was behind the plain fields. Photograph from Benson J. Lossing's The Pictorial Field-Book of the Revolution

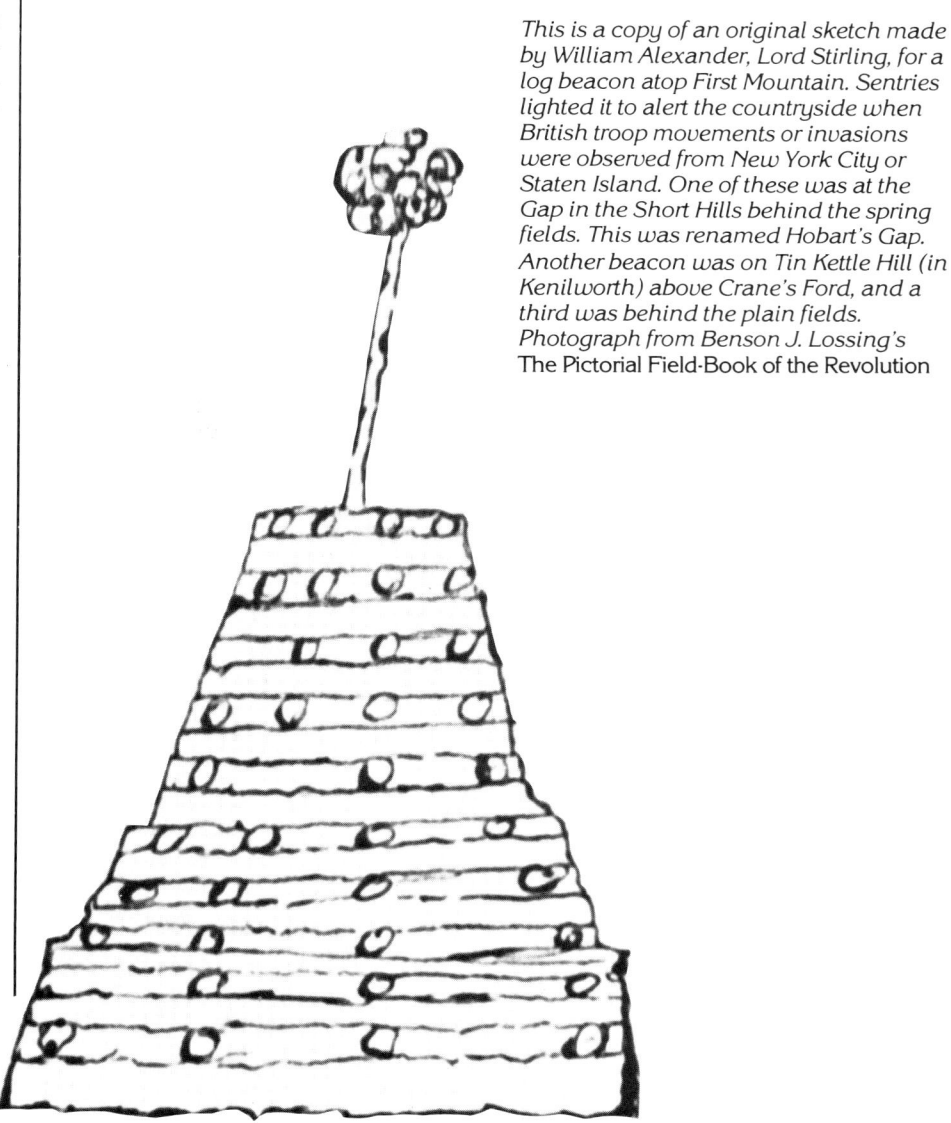

Governor William Livingston wrote for the patriotic cause under pseudonyms. Photograph courtesy of the Elizabeth Public Library

Shepard Kollock, a printer, was serving with the Continental army at Morristown when General Henry Knox asked him to start a newspaper to combat the propaganda in the Loyalist papers being published in New York City and being distributed in New Jersey. The first issue of the New Jersey Journal, *forerunner of the* Daily Journal, *was printed on February 16, 1779, at Chatham. Kollock later moved to New Brunswick. In 1785 he located in Elizabethtown. He also operated a profitable printing business. Many books contain his imprint. The paper was known as the Voice of the Revolution. In 1890 it merged with the* Elizabeth Daily Journal, *now the* Daily Journal. *Photograph courtesy of the Elizabeth Public Library*

fell back to a mile of Briant's Tavern, lighted fires, and lay on their arms. It was expected that the battle would resume at dawn. At sunrise, Colonel Ford found that the British, like the Arabs, had folded their tents and silently stolen away. The militia pursued them to the west fields but it was too late. Hatfield writes in *History of Elizabeth, N. J.,* "This was the first instances in the state of New Jersey when British troops turned their backs and fled from those they called rebels, and this success, small as the affair was, taught the Jersey militia that the foe was not invincible."

The success at the spring fields was followed December 26 by Washington's surprise party for the Hessians at Trenton. The sad and gloomy days early in the month turned to gladness as the patriots were fired with an indomitable zeal for victory.

The Battle of Trenton caused the Hessians at Elizabethtown to be on constant alert. "The good times are over. We do not disrobe when we retire," Philip Waldeck, a chaplain with the Third Hessian Regiment of Bremerlee, Germany, wrote. Earlier in his diary, he described Elizabethtown as "an earthly paradise of cleared woods and beautiful orchards, by the most fertile, productive and richly cultivated lands." He was billeted in the home of a coppersmith, a Loyalist, whose wife was a rebel.

The Continental militia captured thirty baggage wagons and 1,000 bushes of salt in Spanktown in a well-executed raid on the exposed British-Hessian forces. This harassment of the British by the Continental forces in the spring fields, Newark Town, Elizabethtown, and Spanktown area apparently was too much for the British. The 1,600 Hessians and Highlanders moved back to Amboy on January 9, 1777, six weeks after the occupation began.

The British and Hessian forces based at Amboy attempted to draw General Washington into battle on the plains before the Short Hills in June 1777. General William Lord Howe advanced as far as Somerset County Courthouse, while General Washington's sentries watched from atop the Watchung Mountains and his troops waited at Middlebrook.

Frederic C. Detwiller in his book, *War in the Countryside,* estimated that some 20,000 troops were involved in the cat and mouse maneuvering. The British were stopped at Bloody Gap above the Scotch Plains and retreated to Amboy, maliciously burning farms along the route.

Throughout the hostilities, British and Hessian troops made frequent forays into Elizabethtown for supplies and in one instance even attempted to capture Governor Livingston. When they failed, they burned the courthouse and the First Presbyterian Church.

In June 1780 the British, encouraged by reports of mutiny and privation among the Continental forces camped at Jockey Hollow, mounted a major campaign. They hoped to capture Washington's supplies and to cut the Jersey corridor for use by Continental forces. (Some observers also add that the action was designed to keep Washington in New Jersey, while the main British army engaged in major campaigns in Georgia and the Carolinas.)

General Wilhelm Knyphausen, with 5,000 to 6,000 men, landed at Elizabethtown Point (the Gateway to New Jersey) on June 6, 1780. He formed two columns and marched one up the New Point Road and the other up the Old Point Road (now First Avenue). They were met at the Crossroads by twelve pickets, stationed there by Colonel Elias Dayton, the rebel commander. Moses Ogden, the leader, aimed and fired, mortally wounding General Thomas Stirling, the column leader, and knocking him off his horse. The British advance was halted while Stirling was carried to the rear. Nineteen-year-old Moses was killed later that day at Connecticut Farms.

While the enemy was attending General Stirling, the rebel drums were beating the alarm. Old Sow, the cannon, at the Gap in the Short Hills was fired, and the beacon, known as Signal 10, was lighted.

The British regrouped and marched as far as the Connecticut Farms church. The rebel militia by this time was aroused and harassed the British along the way. General William Maxwell drove the first units back at the Farms church. The British pressed and pushed forward. The militia kept arriving. By nightfall, the rebels had driven the British back again.

It was during this retreat that Hannah Ogden Caldwell, wife of Reverend James Caldwell, pastor of the Elizabethtown Presbyterian Church and chaplain for the Third Battalion, was shot in the Connecticut Farms Presbyterian Church parsonage. According to the testimony taken after the killing of Hannah Caldwell, when the fighting began, she was in the house with a young girl, a servant woman and two children, one a baby in arms. The shooting by a red-coated soldier is considered deliberate. She was hit twice. Soldiers then set fire to the house. Her body was carried to the Wade house nearby. She was buried the next day in the churchyard.

The British-Hessian forces retreated to their positions at Elizabethtown Point through a severe thunderstorm. The next day, June 8, they were attacked by units commanded by Brigadier General Edward Hand. The action was a stalemate, and the enemy remained locked in at "the Point" for about two weeks. On June 23, 1780, they attempted the feat again.

General George Washington received word about the same time that General Sir Henry Clinton, British commander, was sailing north from South Carolina with 12,000 men. Fearing the British planned to attack West Point, General Washington placed General Nathanael Greene in charge of the troops at Morristown and began marching north.

The British quickly advanced past Connecticut Farms as the guns fired and the beacon blazed. They divided into two columns; one followed the Vauxhall Road and the other the future Morris Turnpike. Major "Light Horse" Harry Lee, who had been ordered from Philadelphia by General Washington, was placed near Little's Bridge over the Rahway River on the Vauxhall Road along with Captain George Walker and Colonel Mathias Ogden. Colonel Dayton was directed to defend the bridge on the main road. Brigadier General John Stark and Brigadier General William Maxwell were stationed in the "Heights above the mill" (Fleming, *The Forgotten Victory*).

Colonel Israel Angell's force of less than 200 men guarded the first bridge into the tiny hamlet, while Colonel Israel Shreve was behind him at a second bridge. Soldiers ripped up the planking on the first bridge to slow the advancing British.

Colonels Dayton and Angell fought desperately for more than a half hour on the main road. The single field-piece on a small hill nearby (later named Battle Hill) harassed the enemy. During the heat of the battle, the troops ran out of wadding for their muskets. Reverend James Caldwell, their chaplain, ran to the nearby Spring Fields Presbyterian Church and seized hymnals by Reverend Isaac Watts for wadding. Distributing them to the soldiers, he urged, "Now put Watts into them Boys!" This is considered one of the most heroic stories of the war and is a subject of a poem by Brett Hart.

The British crossed the Vauxhall Road bridge but were forced to withdraw at the main bridge. Abandoning the fight, the British withdrew and retreated to the Arthur Kill. Sloops were anchored across the Kill. Planks were placed on top of them, creating a makeshift bridge. Soldiers and horses hurried across it to Staten Island.

The war continued until the British sailed out of New York Harbor in 1783, but this was the last major action in the North. All other action was in the form of raids. If the British had been able to force their way through the gap, the war might have ended differently. The Knyphausen-Clinton ploy had failed. It was defeated by the heroic stand of the Continental line and an aroused militia protecting its home.

The gate to the corridor of New Jersey was closed. ∎

General Elias Dayton served in the French and Indian War and commanded the force that went to Lord Stirling's aid in the capture of the Blue Mountain Valley. By war's end, General Dayton was the highest-ranking officer in New Jersey. Photograph from W. Woodtord Clayton's History of Union and Middlesex Counties

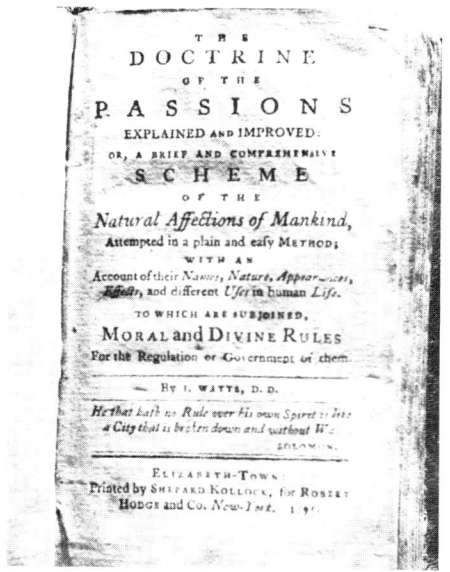

This is the title page of one of the many books printed by Shepard Kollock, who after the Revolutionary War operated a printing business in New Brunswick, New York, and Elizabethtown. Photograph by Richard T. Koles

View of Liberty Hall, the home of Governor William Livingston and the Kean family. Photograph courtesy of Mrs. John Kean

The Cavalier Jouet mansion (now in Roselle) was one of two owned by Jouet, a Tory. Jouet fled to England during the Revolutionary War. He became an Anglican priest while in England. When he returned to the United States after the war, he was not accepted by the community, and he went back to England. The house now is owned by Mr. and Mrs. Charles L. Aquilina. Photograph by Charles L. Aquilina

Leslie's Popular Monthly in December 1879 depicted the murder of Hannah Ogden Caldwell in this manner. Others believe that she was seated on a bed with one of her two children in her arms. Testimony taken after her death would indicate she was inside the house, not outside as shown on the county's shield. Photograph courtesy of the Rahway Historical Society

Washington's headquarters during the Revolutionary War in Rawack (Rahway). This site was used by Quinn and Boden, book publishers, until 1978, when the plant was closed. Photograph courtesy of the Roselle Public Library

This map shows the campaign in Rahway in 1777. Map courtesy of F. Alexander and Robin J. Shipley

Women, as well as men, helped to fight the Revolutionary War in Union County. This strip by Frank Thorne describes how Rachael French outwitted a group of Redcoats. Strip courtesy of Frank Thorne

The old Wood house in Linden was built between Rahway and Elizabethtown prior to the Revolutionary War. Photograph (circa 1870) courtesy of the Linden Public Library

Cast in 1873 at the Meneely Bell Foundry, West Troy, New York, the New Providence Liberty Bell or old Academy Bell was used to call children to classes for thirty-four years in New Providence Township and Borough. It was also used to announce special events until 1945, when the bell rope broke while V-J Day, which ended World War II, was being proclaimed.

The bell was taken down in 1964, displayed briefly at the opening of New Providence High School on September 9, 1964, and is now kept at the Historical Society Museum. The cupola for the bell was built in 1870. The Academy was the first public school in that area of the Passaic Valley. All but the kindergarten and first grade (which were moved in 1910) were moved to Lincoln School in 1907. The New Providence Borough Council purchased the school for one dollar in 1917 and converted it for use as the Borough Hall. Bells such as this were used to alert the public during colonial times. Photograph courtesy of Frank W. Orleans

The Old Chateau on Rahway Avenue, Elizabeth, is one of two houses owned by Cavalier Jouet, the Loyalist, that were confiscated during the Revolutionary War. It was subsequently occupied by Oliver F. Spencer, a son-in-law of General Jonathan Dayton, and used as a boys' school by Julius A. Fay. Photograph courtesy of the Elizabeth Public Library

This is the Presbyterian Church, of the spring fields, from which Reverend James Caldwell took the hymnals and urged the troops to use the paper in the hymnals for wadding in their rifles. Photograph by Richard T. Koles

Aaron Ogden began his public career in the Revolutionary War serving as a colonel. He became the state's fifth governor. He also was selected as the first president of the State Bank of Elizabethtown, 1812-1818 (now the National State Bank, Elizabeth). He was given exclusive rights to operate a steam ferry between New Jersey and New York by the state legislature. Thomas Gibbons, who wanted to operate a ferry, challenged him in court. Chief Justice John Marshall ruled in favor of Gibbons, observing that the federal government, not the states, had jurisdiction over interstate commerce. Photograph courtesy of the National State Bank, Elizabeth

The reputation of Jonathan Dayton, the signer of the Constitution, was stained by the scandals that surrounded his friend, Aaron Burr, Jr., but Dayton was never placed on trial. Photograph from W. Curtis Taylor and Company, Philadelphia; courtesy of the Alexander Library, Rutgers University

Martha Washington, wife of General Washington, visited Elizabethtown several times. The first was in 1776, when she traveled to Boston, Massachusetts to be with him. She attended the wedding of Catherine Smith and Elisha Boudinot, and she was a guest of Governor and Mrs. William Livingston at Liberty Hall in April 1789, when she went to New York City to become the nation's first lady. Postcard of painting by Gilbert Stuart from Charles Aquilina's collection

45

The Kenilworth Inn was built prior to the Revolutionary War. It was used as a private home until the 1890s, when it became the Union House Hotel. It stood on the Boulevard at North Twentieth Street, until it was torn down in the 1940s. Photograph courtesy of the Kenilworth Historical Society

Washington used this old house in Fanwood as headquarters. Postcard (circa 1907) courtesy of the Fanwood Public Library

The Continental troops removed planks from bridges in an effort to slow the British advance. This representation was drawn by William Nichol of the Springfield Historical Society. Drawing from Charles L. Aquilina's June, 1780. The Battles for Springfield, New Jersey: A Comparison of Human Interest Accounts

The old Stage House Inn in Scotch Plains was old when Marquis de Lafayette dined there with friends. George Washington was probably one of Lafayette's friends. He is said to have passed the inn many times. The inn was one of the stagecoach stops on the Old York Road, hence its name. It is now operated as a restaurant. The pole in front is a modern version of the Liberty Pole. The cannon is a World War I version. Photograph by Richard T. Koles

The Central Railroad of New Jersey and the Pennsylvania Railroad crossed at grade in Elizabeth when this photograph was taken on October 25, 1889. The crossings were hazardous to the trains, carriages, and people that traveled through the area, and the trains caused much traffic congestion. Photograph from the Charles L. Aquilina's collection

CHAPTER IV
1785-1865

TRAILS TO TRAINS

This tintype by Warren B. Crater of Roselle Park, made in 1875, shows Central Railroad of New Jersey Engine No. 22, built by Baldwin Locomotive Company in January 1870. It was known as the Camel. *The engineer was John V. Wait of Elizabethport. Photograph courtesy of the Roselle Park Historical Society*

The years after the signing of the Treaty of Paris were busy ones for residents of Elizabethtown. Residents who had fled to safety behind First and Second mountains during the hostilities returned to their communities to restore their dwellings and schools, raise barns, drive fence posts, and replace fences, replant gardens, and participate in lotteries to raise money to reconstruct burned churches.

Elias Dayton, the new state's highest-ranking military officer at war's end, declined the proposal that he be a representative to the Constitutional Convention, urging that his eldest son, Jonathan, be sent in his place. Elias preferred to stay in Elizabethtown and tend to his mercantile business neglected by him during seven years of war.

The government, in its turn on local, state, and national levels, had to transform temporary unions into permanent ones. Elias Boudinot, who had served as commissioner general of prisoners during the war, was selected as president of the Continental Congress during 1781-83. Since he signed the peace treaty with England, many historians consider him the first president of the United States. He also issued the first presidential proclamation for Thanksgiving Day on the second Thursday of December 1783.

Abraham Clark, the signer of the Declaration of Independence, served in the First and Second Continental Congresses and was on a committee to write the constitution. Governor William Livingston, who continued in that office until his death in 1790, and Jonathan Dayton approved the constitution on September 17, 1787.

April 23, 1789, was a banner day. George Washington, president-elect, and his party traveled through present-day Union County from Bridgetown or Lower Rahway to Elizabethport enroute

Cranford's first railroad depot (left), built about 1864, was referred to as French House, because one of seven dwellings within a mile of the railroad station was owned by a Frenchman. Some children visiting Josiah Crane's home nearby, printed the word Craneville *on a shack near the railroad. The new name stuck. When the township was formed in 1871, the founders selected Cranford in place of New Brooklyn, the name suggested by the railroad. In 1865 the little building was joined by the one at the right. It continued to stand until about 1905, when it was replaced by the new station. Photograph courtesy of the Cranford Historical Society*

to New York City, where he took the oath of office as the president of the United States. After spending the night in Woodbridge, he was honored at an inn along the Road to Elizabethtown in Rawack and stopped at Samuel Smith's Tavern in Elizabethtown for refreshments. His last stop before embarkation was for lunch at the home of Elias Boudinot. Guests at the luncheon included some of the most outstanding men in the new nation: Henry Knox of Maine, the secretary of war; John Jay of New York, first chief justice of the United States Supreme Court; his father-in-law, Governor William Livingston of New Jersey; Richard Henry Lee of Virginia; and Charles Carroll of Maryland. The Boudinots used their best china and silver settings. After the luncheon, the procession continued to Elizabethport, where thirteen young women, representing each of the thirteen states, welcomed the new chief executive of the nation. Washington boarded a barge rowed by thirteen oarsmen dressed in white for the trip to New York City. Cheering crowds lined the road and docks to watch Washington pass.

Young Colonel Aaron Ogden moved into the Belcher-Ogden mansion on East Jersey Street, resuming his law practice at war's end. He served in the United States Senate in 1801 and was Essex County clerk. He became the state's fifth governor on his peace platform on the eve of the War of 1812, considered by some to be the second war for independence. He left office after a single year. The state legislature granted him exclusive rights to operate ferries between Elizabethtown and New York City. Thomas Gibbons challenged these rights in court. Chief Justice John Marshall, in a landmark decision, declared that only Congress has the power to regulate interstate commerce, not the states.

The Lyon's Farms School was built from stone cut in a local quarry, and Captain David Lyon helped organize the North End School in Elizabethtown. The Quakers in Rahway and Plainfield, who had been conducting school in homes, built more suitable buildings.

There was a need for coins. The new government directed that three mints, two in present-day Union County, meet this need. One was located on the west bank of the Rahway River of the Upper Road to Rahway and the other in Elizabethtown in a room behind the kitchen at Matthias Ogden's house off the Road to the Courthouse, also called the Road to Elizabethtown Point.

The copper coins contained a horse head above a plowshare, which symbolized the agricultural community, and contained the Latin words *Nova Caesarea* for New Jersey and the Latin slogan *E Pluribus Unum*, meaning "one nation out of many states."

The Elizabethtown Post Office, established in 1775, was one of the first in the nation. Since there was no delivery of letters, the names of recipients were posted in a known spot. After the *New Jersey Journal* moved to the borough, the names were listed in the newspaper. At first the cost of sending a letter by stagecoach depended upon the distance. In 1851 the system of weighing letters was introduced.

Although there was some stagecoach service before the Revolutionary War, the era of the stagecoach and stagecoach lines followed the war. In 1782 Ichabod Grumman, who had been a courier during the war, and James Drake announced in the *New Jersey Journal* that a stage wagon drawn by four horses suitable for carrying passengers would be operating from Elizabethtown to Princeton at 8 a.m. every Tuesday and Thursday. The price for the trip was four dollars. Baggage up to 150 pounds also would cost four dollars. This stagecoach line was the original Swiftsure and Speedwell Line. It was later extended to Philadelphia and Pittsburgh. It received a government contract to carry the mails. The Grummans quartered 200 horses on their property in Lyon's Farms.

In 1787 two rival stagecoach lines owned by Benjamin Friedman and George O'Hara, respectively, began operating between Morristown and Elizabethtown Point, where both lines met the New York-bound boats. Another stage line originating in Morristown crossed Hobart's Gap and made stops at Springfield, Vaux Hall, and Newark Town. Hobart's Gap was named for Bishop John Henry Hobart, who purchased land around the Gap in the Short Hills before he founded Hobart College in Geneva, New York, in 1822.

Elizabethtown became the center for the leather industry. Tanners prepared leather for saddles, bridles, harnesses, and shoes. Carriages were made in Rahway and Elizabethtown. Carriage springs, wheels, and spokes also were made.

The condition of the roads was poor. Much of the time the roads were impassable. Wheels of wagons and carriages became mired in mud in wet weather. Ruts in dry weather gave a jouncy, unpleasant ride. More than once passengers were required to push a vehicle out of the mud or walk to the top of a hill to lighten the load for the horses.

Communication was poor between Elizabethtown and its outlying hamlets. The farmers in New Providence, Rahway, Springfield, Connecticut Farms, and Westfield disliked taking the trip to the center of Elizabethtown to conduct their business or pay their taxes. Soon they formed their own municipalities to better serve their needs.

The need for better communication caused the formation of canal and turnpike companies in the early 1800s. None of the canals cut through present-day Union County. The new Morris Turnpike, completed in 1804, followed the old road between Morristown and Elizabethtown. Unlike other roads in the area, it was thirty-four feet wide, wide enough for two wagons traveling in opposite directions to pass each other. Tolls were collected at pikes placed across the road about every five miles. The new road was used by the Morristown and Elizabeth Stage Company, by peddlers in wagons or on foot, by farmers to carry their produce, and to drive cattle, sheep, and hogs to market. Unapproved roads grew around several of the turnpike's toll gates. They were called "shun pikes" because people used them to avoid paying the toll. Shunpike Road in Springfield started as one of them.

Several laws were adopted by the new state legislature to improve the lot of slaves. No vessel could engage in the slave trade, and no additional slaves could be brought into the state. Slaves and mulattoes were to be judged for crimes on the same basis as white

The Williams-Droescher Mill at Cranford is said to have produced blankets for the troops during the Revolutionary War. Other records indicate that it was built about 1812 and used as a gristmill. Severin R. Droescher used the mill site to manufacture razor hones and tool stones. He served on the Union County Board of Freeholders for many years. The mill pond area is part of the Union County park system. The mill is now occupied by offices. Photograph by Richard T. Koles

51

Seeley's Paper Mills on Green Brook at Scotch Plains circa 1875. Photograph by Guillermo Thorn; courtesy of the Hatfield family

The Parkhurst Mill on Mill Lane, Westfield, (Mountainside) made paper. The mill pond is now Echo Lake.

Photograph courtesy of the Westfield Historicla Society

men, and slaves born after 1788 had to be taught to read and write at the master's expense before they were twenty-one years old. The Gradual Abolition Act was adopted in 1804. Anybody born after July 4, 1804, would be freed at twenty-five years if a male and at twenty-one years if a female. Slavery was abolished in the state in 1844.

The steam engine, long dreamed about, was perfected by Robert Fulton in 1807 and used in his first steamboat on the Hudson River. The same principles were soon adopted by railroads. Two railroad companies began building tracks through Elizabethtown. They were the Elizabethtown and Somerville Railroad (later the Central Railroad of New Jersey) and the New Jersey Railroad and Transportation Company (later the Pennsylvania Railroad). The first passenger service on the Elizabethtown and Somerville Railroad to Plainfield started on January 1, 1839. Within the decade it went to Easton, Pennsylvania. Service to Rahway from Elizabethtown on the New Jersey Railroad began in 1835 and to the Summit on Delaware and Lackawanna and Western Railroad in 1837.

The railroad opened the farm land to developers, residences, business and, in the future, industry. Lumber and coal companies and other small establishments located on nearby sidings, and communities grew around the railroad mail stations. The railroads brought city people into the area on outings, vacations, and to live. The commuter was born.

The Elizabethtown Water Company was founded in 1855 to provide pure water to replace water taken from the contaminated wells. The Elizabethtown Gas Company was founded the same year to provide gas for lights in the houses. Candles and lanterns still were used in the farm areas. That same year, Elizabethtown officials decided that the old borough form of government was unable to provide modern needs, and the city was organized. The formation of the city, led to the final break with Essex County.

The steam engine, which powered the ferry boats and the locomotives, was soon being applied to factories. Among the first and largest of these was the Elizabeth Cordage Company, known by Elizabethans as "the rope walk." Fronting on the Elizabeth River on twenty acres of land, it had its own wharfs, machine shops, spinning department, rope walk, and a park with a lake. It opened in 1829 and employed 1,000 people. The mill portion was damaged by fire on June 24, 1880, and rebuilt that year. A second fire on March 17, 1891, leveled the rope works.

Other early businesses were the John Curtis, later the John Carroll, brick works, started in 1850, where bricks were made from the extensive clay beds along the Arthur Kill, the foundry of Charles E. and Samuel L. Moore, later the S. L. Moore and Sons Company, known as the Crescent Iron Works. Organized in 1854, it made iron castings such as those used in fences and railroad gates at crossings, ore crushers and pulverizers, and various types of machines. Keen Pruden founded a pottery in 1835 on the banks of the Elizabeth River to manufacture red earthenware. L. B. Beerbower Elizabeth Pottery Company succeeded him and made decorated ware. Shipbuilding at Elizabethport was a major industry, which continued during the pre-Civil War period. In 1849 the Rutan, Colon and Crowell Company, located on Marshall Street and the Elizabeth River, was building three-masted schooners.

Despite these strides, most of Union County continued to be rural until well after the Civil War. The Civil War took ten companies of residents from the county. Aged Elizabeth resident, General Winfield Scott, the hero of the War of 1812 and the Mexican War, was briefly placed in command of the Union forces. Troops paraded on the old parade grounds on Broad Street. Local industries geared for wartime

French's Mill was built in 1853 at 20-32 Somerset Street in Plainfield. It provided power for the first electric lights in Plainfield. Photograph courtesy of the Plainfield Public Library

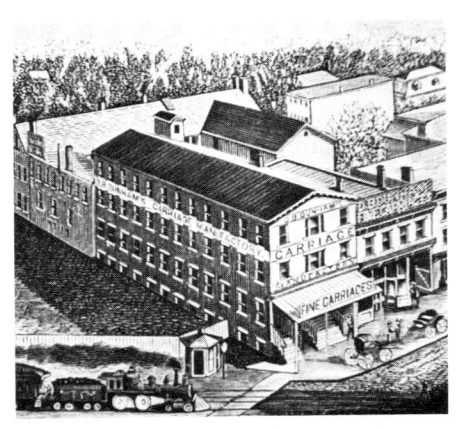

Rahway and Elizabethtown became centers for the manufacture of carriages after the turn of the nineteenth century. The new railroad, which soon would put the carriage manufacturers out of business, was located near D. B. Dunham's Carriage Manufactory in Rahway. Photograph from W. Woodtord Clayton's History of Union and Middlesex Counties

production. A carriage maker in Rahway was given a government contract to construct 100 wagons and the same number of ambulances. J. A. Bannister of Elizabeth was ordered to make 100,000 pairs of shoes for the soldiers.

Women in Elizabeth organized the Union Aid Society in June 1861 and opened its headquarters over the Tucker and Ogden's Store at 160 Broad Street. Women came to the office between 9 a.m. and 6 p.m. every Thursday to pick up their sewing assignments to make clothing for the servicemen and the patients at the army hospital in Newark. Other women at Salem (Union Township-Hillside Township) collected clothes for the patients. Pierson Brothers' Store, also on Broad Street, became a depository for articles which were then given to people in hospitals.

Measles and yellow typhoid fever killed many of the soldiers in the Virginia camps and their families at home. Heroic deeds, victories, and diaries of servicemen were described in the area's newspapers. Four of the men were awarded the Congressional Medal of Honor. Three of these men are buried in Evergreen Cemetery, Hillside. They are J. Madison Drake of Elizabeth, later publisher of several newspapers; Captain William Brant of Elizabeth; and Major Rufus King, who enlisted in the Seventh Regiment of the New York Volunteers at the beginning of the war and settled in Union Township (Pingry School site in Hillside) at war's end. The fourth was Julian Scott, a drummer boy from Plainfield.

Although farming continued to be the major interest after the war, Union County was on the verge of the industrial revolution. ■

Elizabeth Crane Day was the youngest child of Aunt Betsy Mulford Crane, who kept a diary. The diary provides a glimpse of life in New Providence (Berkeley Heights) in the 1820s. Photograph courtesy of the Berkeley Heights Historical Society

Captain Townley's mushroom farm and house located at the Union Township-Elizabeth line. The house was built circa 1830. Photograph courtesy of the Newark Public Library

One of the old mills in Feltville, where David Felt published books and manufactured writing paper and other paper products. Photograph by Quillermo Thorn; courtesy of the Hatfield family

This is one of the six cottages still standing in Feltville, Union County's first company town. Feltville was founded in 1844 by David Felt, a New York businessman and publisher. Felt put a dam across Blue Brook to create a reservoir and began operating a paper mill and printing business. Part of the lake is preserved as Surprise Lake in Watchung Reservation. Photograph by Richard T. Koles

A winter scene on the Arthur Kill, circa 1875. Photograph from Harper's Weekly, 1875; courtesy of Zara Cohan

This building served as the church, school, and general store for the community of Feltville. The village was deserted after Felt died on April 17, 1860. Dr. Samuel P. Townsend attempted to grow fruit and tobacco and raise horses at the site. He failed. Warren Ackerman restored the area and operated Glenside Park, a summer resort, from 1882 to 1916, when it was deserted again. This building now serves as the headquarters for the Union Outdoor Education Center. Photograph by Richard T. Koles

Irving Street, Rahway, looked this way before the railroad was elevated, creating a "Chinese wall" through Rahway. Photograph (1859) courtesy of the Rahway Historical Society

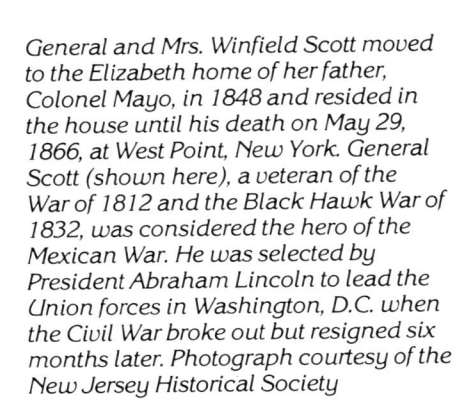

General and Mrs. Winfield Scott moved to the Elizabeth home of her father, Colonel Mayo, in 1848 and resided in the house until his death on May 29, 1866, at West Point, New York. General Scott (shown here), a veteran of the War of 1812 and the Black Hawk War of 1832, was considered the hero of the Mexican War. He was selected by President Abraham Lincoln to lead the Union forces in Washington, D.C. when the Civil War broke out but resigned six months later. Photograph courtesy of the New Jersey Historical Society

55

The house in which the Scotts lived stood in East Jersey Street and Madison Avenue, Elizabeth, until 1931, when it was removed for a gasoline station. Scott is remembered in Scott Park, currently opposite the house. Photograph courtesy of the New Jersey Historical Society

Staff and guests all appeared outside for the photo session at Laing's Hotel, West Front Street, Plainfield, about 1865. Laing's was just one of several hotels in Union County where city people vacationed. Photograph courtesy of the Plainfield Public Library

This Civil War recruiting poster is on display in the Drake house at Plainfield. Photograph by Richard T. Koles

The most poignant monument to the Civil War is in the Presbyterian Church cemetery in Springfield near the Millburn line, where William and Elias Poole, brothers, are buried. They served on opposite sides during the War Between the States. Photograph courtesy of the Newark Public Library

General J. Madison Drake of Elizabeth, publisher of the Sunday Leader, Elizabeth Daily Leader, *and the* Daily Monitor *was one of the Union County recipients of the Congressional Medal of Honor for his actions in the Civil War. He organized the Veterans Zouaves, which became one of the most famous drill teams in the nation. From Drake's* Historical Sketches of the Revolutionary and Civil Wars; *photograph by Richard T. Koles*

Julian Scott of Plainfield rescued eleven of his fellow soldiers from the swollen waters of the Warwick River in Virginia in 1862. He was presented the first medal of honor struck in the Civil War. Photograph courtesy of the National Archives

The years after the Civil War were years of great expectations in Union County. Many wealthy people from New York City built "summer cottages" in Plainfield and Summit and other sections of the county. The mansions and their furnishings rivaled the castles in Europe. Here is a cross-section from homes of some of Plainfield's fifty millionaires. This was the hallway in the home of William Palmer Smith. Photograph courtesy of the Newark Public Library

Library of the Charles Potter home. Photograph courtesy of the Newark Public Library

CHAPTER V
1865-1900
GREAT EXPECTATIONS

Entrance hall of the Charles W. McCutcheon home. Photograph courtesy of the Newark Public Library

The Civil War moved Union County into the industrial revolution. Until the Civil War, only Elizabeth, of Union County's first seven municipalities, had varied industries. There were small forges and foundries to make cooking stoves, furnaces, and other articles. There were lumber and coal yards, print shops, tanneries, shoe manufacturers, and shipyards.

Carriages were made in Elizabeth and Rahway. Hatters were abundant in Plainfield. A small woolen factory was located near Barnett's Mills (Clark) in Rahway. Shoes were made in Rahway. The communities boasted dry goods stores, a variety of mills, blacksmiths, taverns, churches, and craftsmen to make such articles as clocks and furniture.

When the railroads were built, speculators began buying up farms in their vicinity. The first of these was Edward N. Kellogg of New York City, who purchased land from the waterfront to Seventh Street from the river to Pine Street in 1835. He subdivided the land into house lots for the New Manufacturing Town of Elizabethport to accommodate workers in anticipated industries. The lots were 25 by 100 feet each.

Another developer was Jonathan Crane Bonnel, "father of modern-day Summit." Bonnel, proprietor of a sawmill on the Passaic River, purchased the 200-acre farm of Jonathan Potter on the Summit of First Mountain. He offered the Morris and Essex Railroad (Delaware, Lackawanna and Western Railroad) a right of way through his property and even promised to build a depot near the store of his son-in-law, William Littell. The railroad accepted the offer. The first locomotive, the *Orange,* reached the Summit in August 1837. The 200-acre farm became Summit's business district.

Realizing the attraction of the mountaintop, Bonnel built the first hotel in 1858. He called it the Summit House.

The new millionaires and their associates enjoyed the "sport of kings." There were several race tracks within the county, including tracks in Plainfield, Elizabeth, and Westfield. This is the Fair Acres Race Track, Westfield. Photograph courtesy of the Westfield Historical Society

The James E. Martine home in Plainfield was known as Cedar Brook Farm. Built prior to the Revolutionary War, the house continues to be a private residence. Photograph (circa 1876) by Guillermo Thorn of Plainfield; courtesy of the Hatfield family

This hotel burned in 1867, but it had served its purpose. Many former summer and seasonal guests purchased land and built homes, first for vacation use and later for permanent use. George Manley, for instance, purchased twenty-eight-acres in 1859 on which the Rosary Shrine and Manley Court Apartments stand. James Riera, the first developer, purchased the thirty-eight-acre Noe farm in 1858 and subdivided it into Riera Park. Other entrepreneurs formed the Central Land Improvement Company in the future Fanwood and Samuel Garwood's Land Improvement Company.

The developments were accompanied by stores to supply consumer goods and demands for services such as electric lights, gas for cooking, water supply systems, and sewers. The newcomers built stately mansions surrounded by beautiful gardens with fountains, gazebos, and trees. Many of them could be compared favorably with the manor houses and castles in Europe. In fact, Plainfield, where fifty millionaires were said to live, was soon called the Queen City. Each mansion used the finest woods, stained-glass windows, marble for fireplaces and floors, glass chandeliers, and wrought-iron trim. Each one contained the most recent inventions and gadgets of the age.

Meanwhile in Elizabeth, I. M. Singer, manufacturer of sewing machines, purchased land on Newark Bay, where he consolidated his operations. The company, opened in 1873, was the leading manufacturer of sewing machines for home use in the world for more than 100 years. The company's labor force of more than 6,000 persons was the largest in the world.

Thomas Grasselli opened the Grasselli Chemical Company on Tremley Point in Linden in 1888. Russell Coe had a bone and acid works nearby. They were joined by the S. S. Fales and Company Chemical Works; the W. J. Bush Company; the Mountain Copper Company, smelters; Swan, Finch and Company, oil refiners; and Warner Asphalt Company. Others followed rapidly. W. H. Rankin began operating a roofing and sheeting works the same year; the Cooke Brothers made lard, tallow, and oils nearby; the Bowker Fertilizer Company made manures; the Borne Scrymser and Company refined oil; and the T. F. and H. C. Sayre opened a lime, cement, brick, sand, and plaster business.

J. Noah H. Slee began manufacturing a lubricant-polish in 1894 in Rahway. It became the Three-In-One-Oil Company. Gustave Adolph Brachhausen made music boxes in Jersey City in 1892. Four years later he moved his factory to Rahway, where it became the Regina Company, manufacturers of phonographs and vacuum cleaners.

Since the people lived closer together and there were more of them, there was more opportunity to form organizations than before the Civil War. Both Elizabeth and Plainfield became

The First National Bank once stood at 233 Broad Street, Elizabeth. It was destroyed by fire in 1890. This is an original 1869 photograph. Photograph courtesy of the Elizabeth Public Library

known as the City of Churches. The churches began to form church-related groups. In addition there were businessmen groups, fraternal and masonic groups, veterans' groups, library associations, university clubs, riding clubs, canoeing clubs, bicycle clubs, neighborhood civic associations, Y's, and lodges, just to mention a few. Tennis, golf, and yacht clubs were founded. Picnic areas increased. The railroads began running excursions to the Jersey shore, Lake Hopatcong, and the Catskill Mountains.

Musical, art, and literary groups were formed. Individuals began collecting art treasures. Several people were artists, writers, and musicians. Opera houses were built. Stock companies and vaudeville troupes began making regular appearances in the new theaters.

An organized concern began for one's fellowman. Dr. J. Ackerman Coles donated land for the future Children's Specialized Hospital and the Newark Orphanage, both in Mountainside, and Colonel E. H. Ropes donated a farm in Summit for the Fresh Air and Convalescent Home and Arthur Home for Destitute Boys. Hospitals, too, were organized.

Nearly every community had a casino where public balls, lectures, and community festivals were held. The most famous were the river carnivals in Cranford, which became known as the Venice of America.

The splintering of Union County, begun because of different interests and distances from the seats of power, continued after the Civil War. Linden Township was formed in 1861, Clark Township in 1864; Summit Township from New Providence and Springfield in 1869; Cranford from Springfield, Linden, Union, Westfield, and Clark in 1871; Fanwood Township, later Scotch Plains Township, from Plainfield and Westfield in 1887; Roselle Borough from Linden in 1894; Fanwood Borough from Fanwood Township in 1895; and Mountainside from Westfield in 1895. New Providence Borough was cut from New Providence Township, later Berkeley Heights in 1899.

These would be divided into five more communities in the twentieth century: Roselle Park in 1901, Garwood in 1903, Kenilworth in 1907, Hillside in 1913, and Winfield in 1941. ∎

On pleasant days, the people went for rides in their horses and carriages in the countryside or visited each other. Here the Gittels of Park Avenue in Plainfield posed for the photographer before driving forth. Mrs. Gittel used an umbrella to protect her skin from the sun's rays. Photograph by Guillermo Thorn; courtesy of the Hatfield family

In Cranford, the people enjoyed canoeing on the Rahway River, a sport that is still popular today. Photograph (circa 1916) from the Souvenir Program of the Cranford Carnival, July 4, 1916; courtesy of Robert J. Fridlington

Oddly enough, when the exclusive Baltusrol Golf Club in Springfield was built in the 1890s, it selected as its name a corruption of Baltus Roll's name. The U.S. Open Gold Tournament is frequently held on its courses. Photograph courtesy of the Summit Public Library

Baltus Roll was seized by two men during a snowstorm and murdered. The men apparently thought that he had money hidden in the house. Strip courtesy of Frank Thorne

The Tweedy sisters of 125 Crescent Avenue, Plainfield, enjoyed tea. They are (left to right): Tiffany, Belle, Mary, and Florence. The photograph was given to the Plainfield Public Library by Miss Harriet Goddard in December 1971. Photograph courtesy of the Plainfield Public Library

63

The Clio Club in Roselle is one of the oldest women's clubs in New Jersey. Photograph courtesy of the Newark Public Library

John Cummins became the first mayor of Roselle Park Borough in 1901, after it separated from Union Township. Photograph courtesy of the Roselle Park Historical Society

The Scotch Hills Country Club is the only municipally-owned golf course in Union County and one of the few in New Jersey. The clubhouse was the home of John Locey, a farmer, from 1740 to 1800. It was occupied by several other farmers before it became the Westfield Golf Club on Jerusalem Road, circa 1890s. It became the first black country club, the Shady Rest Country Club, owned by a black group in the 1920s. Althea Gibson, the tennis star, played golf and tennis at the club. The township took control of the club in 1964. Photograph courtesy of the Westfield Historical Society

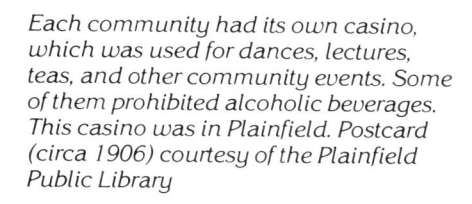

Each community had its own casino, which was used for dances, lectures, teas, and other community events. Some of them prohibited alcoholic beverages. This casino was in Plainfield. Postcard (circa 1906) courtesy of the Plainfield Public Library

Members of the Independent Order of Stars (I.O.S.) posed for the photographer on December 25, 1897. The boy's club was composed of seventeen- and eighteen-year-old youths who participated in sports and conducted social affairs in the old Westfield Club House. Photograph courtesy of the Westfield Historical Society

Summit Public Library, 1891. Photograph courtesy of the Summit Public Library

Mary Ogden White was typical of many well-born women of her time. Daughter of the pastor of the Central Presbyterian Church in Summit, she was active in the Summit Library Association and among the founders of its subscription library. She was also president of the Fortnightly Club, a civic and social group that sponsored charitable activities and projects. Photograph courtesy of the Summit Public Library

Dr. Frederick A. Kinch of Westfield was one of the county's early physicians. Photograph from W. Woodford Clayton's History of Union and Middlesex Counties

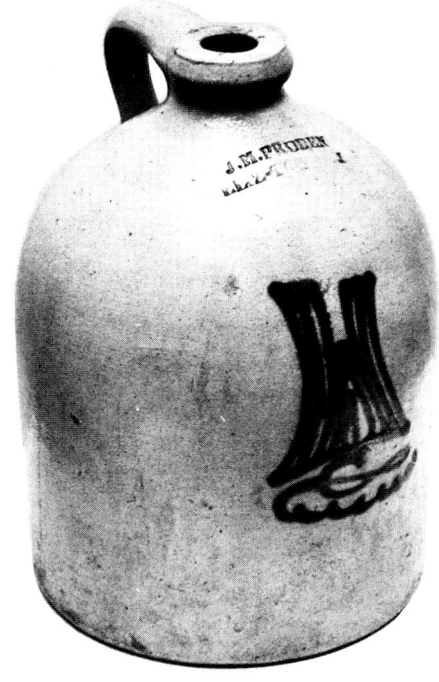

These two jugs, made by J. M. Pruden in Elizabeth, New Jersey, are now owned by Charles L. Aquilina. Photograph by Richard T. Koles

Clay from beds found along the Arthur Kill and the Elizabeth River was used by at least three factories. John Pruden started to manufacture common slip-decorated red earthenware in 1816 on the Elizabeth River at 1122-6 Elizabeth Avenue, near Bridge Street. He called his business the Elizabeth Pottery Works. He was succeeded by his son, Keen (shown here), in 1835. Keen Pruden served in the General Assembly from 1845 to 1846. He became president of the National State Bank, serving from 1851 to 1873, when he resigned. Since then only members of the Kean family have served as the bank's presidents. The L. B. Beerbower Company took over the Pruden works in 1879. Photograph by Richard T. Koles; courtesy of the National State Bank

Beerbower's pottery, circa 1889. Photograph from City of Elizabeth-Illustrated, *1889*

Workmen stood outside a shop in Plainfield about 1880. Photograph by G. Thorn; courtesy of the Hatfield family

Water tower at Kenilworth. It has been replaced by a larger one. Photograph courtesy of the Upsala College Library

Chartered in 1855, the Elizabethtown Gas Light Company provide gas lights to old Elizabethtown from its gas works at the foot of Spring Street and the Elizabeth River. It served 300 customers. In 1982 the company, known as the Elizabethtown Gas Company since 1966, served 192,000 customers in sixty-eight communities in Union, Middlesex, Mercer, Warren, Hunterdon, Sussex, and Morris counties. National Utilities and Industries Company (NUI), formed in 1969, became the parent company of Elizabethtown Gas Company to diversify its interests. Photograph courtesy of the Elizabethtown Gas Company

The Elizabethtown Water Company, founded on March 3, 1854, operated out of this small office (at left) on Broad Street, Elizabeth, until 1882, when the photograph was taken. The building next door at 92 Broad Street was acquired by the new Young Men's Christian Association when it was formed in 1900 and used until 1906, when the first YMCA building was opened at 1136 East Jersey Street.

The water company's water supply came from the Elizabeth River. Soon reservoirs were constructed on Westfield Avenue, Chilton Street, Irvington Avenue, and at Ursino Lake. Icehouses were built on the lake.

The water company supplies about one-fifth of the water currently used by the city of Elizabeth. It also supplies water to customers in Union, Middlesex, and Somerset counties. The water comes from the Raritan River, from wells, and from Round Valley and Spruce Run reservoirs. Photograph courtesy of Kathleen Dunn, YMCA of eastern Union County

The interior of the Essex and Hudson Gas Company, Summit, circa 1900. Photograph courtesy of the Newark Public Library

Thomas Alva Edison has several connections with Union County. He resided with his business partner, Franklin A. Pope, at 235 Morris Avenue, Elizabeth, from September 12, 1869, to April 23, 1870, while he was operating a factory on Edison Place, Newark. It was during this period that he met and married his first wife, Mary Stillwell, one of his employees.

He returned to Union County, searching for a community where he could prove it was both practical and feasible to light an entire village electrically. He rented land from the Roselle Land Improvement Company for a dollar a year. Two wires each were connected with thirty-five dwellings and businesses, including Charlie Stone's grocery store across the railroad tracks in Roselle Park and the First Presbyterian Church, Roselle, where the original chandelier is still in use.

Eleven experimental, mass-produced, low-cost poured-cement houses were built in 1917 on Ingersoll Terrace, Union Township, by Edison and Charles Ingersoll, the dollar watch magnate. They have withstood the test of time and are still standing. Edison's company also made two motion pictures in Kenilworth.

Edison's first electric generating plant was erected on the northeast corner of First Avenue and Locust Street, Roselle. This photograph includes (left to right): Mr. Thomas, fireman and engineer; Charles M. Brooks, manager, and his three-year-old son, Harold; and J. V. Schroeder. The Bachman Veghte Company, headed by Elliot C. Dill, Jr., now occupies the site. Photograph courtesy of William and Ruth Frolich

This tin foil photograph of Thomas A. Edison was taken by Mathew Brady in Washington. Photograph courtesy of the Newark Public Library

The First Presbyterian Church, Roselle, contains the first chandelier wired electrically by the Edison Company for Isolated Light. Photograph of postcard (circa 1900) courtesy of the Roselle Public Library

When Isaac Singer decided to consolidate all his separate sewing machine plants into a single building on a thirty-two-acre plot at the site of Crane's Ferry, he plunged Elizabeth into the industrial revolution. The firm, manufacturers of sewing machines for home use, became the city's largest and major employer and for a time reigned as the largest manufacturing company in the world. The plant was operated in Elizabeth from 1873 to 1982.

The Singer Sewing Machine Company, circa 1889. Photograph from City of Elizabeth-Illustrated

Lebbeus Baldwin Miller, plant manager of the Singer Sewing Machine Company, standardized parts. He became plant manager in 1871 and served until after the turn of the century. Photograph courtesy of Edward L. Fox

Philip Diehl, a native of Germany, was employed as an inventor with the Singer Sewing Machine Company. He also invented the first arc light installed in Elizabeth and an incandescent lamp. He developed a dynamo to provide current for arc lamps, sewing machine motors, and incandescent lamps and held patents on all of them. In 1887 he formed the Diehl Manufacturing Company, manufacturers of electric ceiling fans. He held more than 200 patents. Photograph from A. Van Doren Honeyman's History of Union County

The foundry in the Singer company. Photograph from City of Elizabeth-Illustrated

Singer power machines sewing group. Photograph by Lewis W. Hine, Records of the Work Projects Administration; *from the General Services Administration*

A Singer sewing machine made for home use in 1887. Photograph by Richard T. Koles

The Edward Clark *was named for Isaac M. Singer's partner. Clark, a successful lawyer, served as the company's president from 1875 to 1882. He introduced credit buying. The boat was used to carry sewing machines to New York City. Here the boat is in dry dock at the New Jersey Dry Dock and Transportation Company at the mouth of the Elizabeth River. Photograph from* City of Elizabeth-Illustrated

In 1927, as this photograph shows, trolleys served the thousands of workers at the Singer Manufacturing Company. Prior to the trolley service, Singer employees walked across the meadows to the plant. Photograph courtesy of the Roselle Public Library

71

Ground breaking of a church group in Linden, date unknown. Photograph courtesy of the Linden Public Library

Unlike other religious groups such as the Presbyterians, Anglicans, and Quakers who came through the ports at Elizabethtown and Amboy, the Baptists came into Elizabethtown from Piscataway, where they founded their first church in 1707. They started a church in Scot's Plains, called the First Day Baptist Meeting House on September 8, 1747, now the Scotch Plains Baptist Church. This church, constructed in the 1870s, replaced earlier buildings. The congregation organized a church in Lyon's Farms. The Lyon's Farms church is credited with starting the Baptist churches in Newark and Hillside. Photograph by Richard T. Koles

Old St. Mary's Roman Catholic Church was built on Stony Hill in 1877 and demolished in March 1974. Photograph courtesy of Berkeley Heights Historical Society

The Reformed Church on Wood Avenue at Henry Street in Linden was the new community's first religious sanctuary. Photograph courtesy of the Linden Public Library

The Community United Methodist Church, Roselle Park, spring 1891. Photograph courtesy of the Roselle Park Historical Society

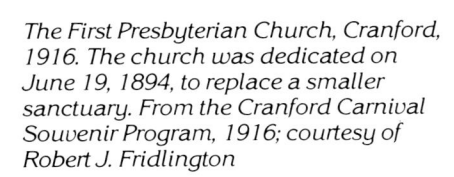

The First Presbyterian Church, Cranford, 1916. The church was dedicated on June 19, 1894, to replace a smaller sanctuary. From the Cranford Carnival Souvenir Program, 1916; courtesy of Robert J. Fridlington

The West Elizabeth railroad station on the Lehigh Valley Railroad about 1895. The station actually was in the Lyon's Farms area of Union Township, now Hillside. The railroad gave it the West Elizabeth name to make people think the railroad serviced Elizabeth. Photograph courtesy of the Newark Public Library

The Pennsylvania Railroad station in Elizabeth with the tracks at ground level before the Arch was built in 1891. Photograph courtesy of the Newark Public Library

Engine stops at the Roselle Park railroad station on the Central Railroad of New Jersey, 1918. Photograph of the Roselle Park Historical Society

In 1894 a group of businessmen from Elmira, New York, formed the New Orange Industrial Association and purchased some thirty farms in Cranford and Union townships. The farms were subdivided into industrial and residential plots. Four factories were erected. Soon the factory owners wanted rail connection. A short line was built between the factories and the Central Railroad at Aldene (Roselle Park) and the Lackawanna Railroad at Summit, a distance of 11.8 miles. There also was a connection with the Lehigh Valley Railroad in Roselle Park. The real estate venture failed. The land was purchased by Levi William Naylor, a native of Kenilworth, England, who renamed it for his home town. Property owners paid their taxes to the company until the borough was formed on May 13, 1907.

When the railroad was taken over by Louis Keller, publisher of The Blue Book, in 1904, he renamed it the Rahway Valley Railroad and built a station near the Baltusrol Golf Club's clubhouse. Passenger service was discontinued in 1919. The railroad, one of the nation's shortest, is one of the most profitable. It is the only railroad that begins and ends in Union County. Photograph courtesy of the Kenilworth Historical Society

The Pennsylvania Railroad station in Linden before the tracks were raised. The railroad caused the formation of two Lindens, which later joined each other. Photograph courtesy of the Linden Public Library

In 1861 Reverend Dr. John F. Pingry, a Presbyterian minister, started the Pingry School in Elizabeth. The school's first classes were held in the home of Jonathan Townley while he was absent with the Union forces in the Civil War. The school was located briefly in the rear of 445 Westminster Avenue, Elizabeth, and on a two-and-a-half-acre tract on Parker Road and Union Avenue, Elizabeth, from 1892 to 1953. It occupied a new complex on North Avenue, Hillside, from 1953 to the 1980s, when it moved to a new 193-acre campus in Bernards Township. The Hillside property was purchased for Kean College of New Jersey in 1981. The school is one of the oldest country day schools.

Dr. John F. Pingry, first headmaster of Pingry School. Photograph courtesy of Pingry School

The Pingry School from 1893 to 1953. The site is now occupied by Elmora School 12, Elizabeth. Photograph courtesy of Pingry School

The original Pingry School in Elizabeth. Photograph courtesy of Pingry School

The 1897 championship football team at Pingry School. Photograph courtesy of Pingry School

Isabel Irving. Photograph courtesy of the Rahway Historical Society

Herbert Ferguson of Cranford stands at attention in his military school uniform in 1897. Photograph courtesy of the Cranford Historical Society

Charles M. and Henry J. Stewart, about 1878. Henry resided at 125 William Street, Roselle, for many years. Charles died in 1894. Photograph courtesy of Alice Elmer

Dr. Charles Davis, who resided in the house now known as the Belcher-Ogden mansion, was a physician, president of the State Bank of Elizabeth from 1840 to 1851, and president of the Elizabethtown Mutual Fire Insurance Company. The State Bank became a national bank on August 1, 1865. Photograph courtesy of the National State Bank, Elizabeth

John H. Kean (1852-1914), son of Colonel John Kean (1814-1895), was elected to Congress in 1882 and 1886 and to the U.S. Senate in 1899 and 1905. He was president of the National State Bank in Elizabeth, of the Elizabethtown Water Company, and of the Elizabethtown Gas Light Company. He founded the Elizabethport Banking Company. Photograph courtesy of the National State Bank, Elizabeth

The National State Bank and the Elizabeth Daily Journal building stood side-by-side in this 1889 photograph. The National State Bank has been at the same site since 1812. The Elizabeth Daily Journal was founded on July 17, 1871, by Frederick W. Foote, owner of the New Jersey Journal. It moved to this location in 1888. In 1924 it moved to a new building at 295 North Broad Street, Elizabeth. Photograph from City of Elizabeth-Illustrated, 1889

Dorothy Fleacke, nee Fischer, as she appeared in this Hopper's Gallery of Art photograph, 1861. Photograph courtesy of the Linden Public Library

Julian H. Kean (1854-1932) succeeded his brother as president of the National State Bank, Elizabeth. He was also president of the Elizabethtown Gas Light Company, president of the Elizabethtown Water Company, and a director of the Elizabethport Banking Company. Photograph courtesy of the National State Bank, Elizabeth

Colonel John Kean (1814-1895) was the first Kean to be elected president of the National State Bank on October 13, 1873. Since then only members of the Kean family have been presidents of the bank. He also was president of the Central Railroad of New Jersey and the Elizabethtown Gas Light Company. At one time, he supervised operation of a glue works which the bank had taken over. Photograph courtesy of the National State Bank

Icehouses of the Elizabeth Ice Company on Ursino Lake. Photograph from City of Elizabeth-Illustrated

The Elizabeth Town and Newark Horse Railway Company on November 1, 1847, announced the operation of a line of omnibuses or trolleys. One horse was used to pull each trolley most of the time. Two horses were used during rush hours. Soon, other trolley lines were started. The first electric car was introduced in 1890. Photograph courtesy of the Newark Public Library

One horse was used to pull each trolley in Cranford. Photograph courtesy of the Cranford Historical Society

A car of the Elizabeth Street Railway Company traveled on the "new line," incorporated in 1888. Photograph from City of Elizabeth-Illustrated, *1889*

North Avenue, Plainfield, circa 1896. Photograph courtesy of the Roselle Public Library

The first store in New Orange (Kenilworth) was built by John Hiller on Washington Avenue at Twenty-First Street in 1898. The store was operated by John's son, Fred. John was the first postmaster and also had a bakery route. He was employed by James Arthur, who was contracted by the Baron Hirsh Company to build 100 houses for its employees. Photograph courtesy of the Kenilworth Historical Society

The Linden Town Hall in 1898. Photograph courtesy of the Linden Public Library

Isaac Lambert's feed store was on North Avenue near the Westfield depot. Lambert is shown standing on the porch. He played the violin at the wedding of John Henry Frazee. Photograph courtesy of John Henry Frazee

Fire was a major concern for early Union County residents. Volunteer fire companies were formed in all areas. The first of these was the Elizabeth Protection Engine Company No. 1, founded in 1837. By 1868 Elizabeth had six volunteer companies, and volunteer companies were being formed in other areas of the county. There was tremendous competition among the companies.

Two white horses pulled the Rahway fire engine circa 1900. Photograph courtesy of the Rahway Historical Society

The four volunteer chiefs in Elizabeth hold trumpets with which to summon their men. The chiefs are (left to right): Joseph O'Neill, William Cox, Cornelius Regan, and James Cummings. Photograph courtesy of the Elizabeth Fire Museum

Elizabeth's Hibernia Volunteer Engine Company No. 5 was composed of Irishmen. Photograph courtesy of the Elizabeth Fire Museum

Bucket and Engine Company No. 1 and Empire Engine Company No. 2, Westfield, circa 1895. Photograph courtesy of the Westfield Historical Society

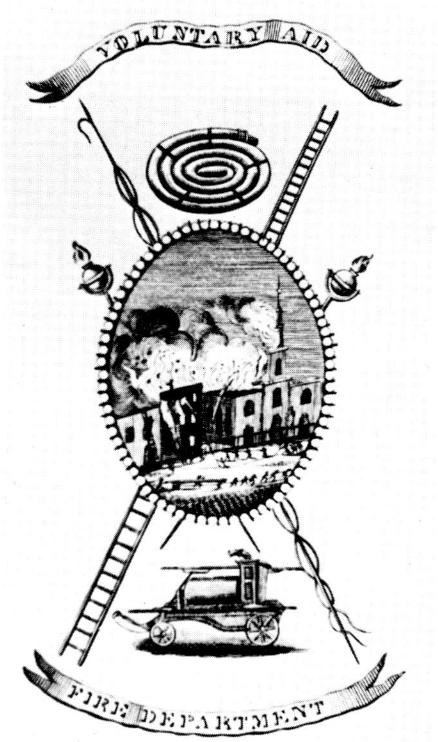

Symbol for the Elizabeth Town Fire Department Voluntary Aid. Photograph courtesy of the Alexander Library, Rutgers University

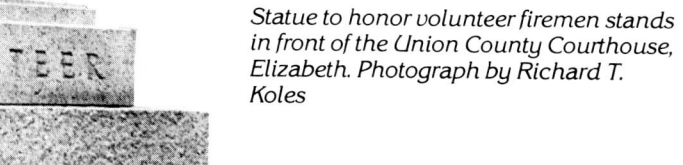

Statue to honor volunteer firemen stands in front of the Union County Courthouse, Elizabeth. Photograph by Richard T. Koles

Soon police departments were being formed throughout Union County. Patrolman Charles Jones (1855-1889) became the first Elizabeth police officer to be killed in the line of duty. Photograph courtesy of Dorothy Salter

This poster seeks information about a young woman who was murdered in Rahway in 1885. She was never identified, and her murderer was never caught. Photograph courtesy of the Rahway Historical Society

John "Jake" Miller served as constable in the Union County court before becoming marshal of the borough of New Providence. Photograph courtesy of the New Providence Historical Society

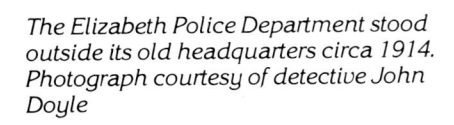

The Elizabeth Police Department stood outside its old headquarters circa 1914. Photograph courtesy of detective John Doyle

83

The Westfield Police Department in the 1890s. Seated left to right: John Knapp, James Harrison. Standing left to right: Thomas O'Neill, Elmer Woodruff, and Captain Cyrus Wilcox. Photograph courtesy of the Westfield Historical Society

Elizabeth Police Captain John J. O'Leary, first president of the New Jersey State Patrolmen's Benevolent Association. Photograph courtesy of the Elizabeth Police Department

John C. Marrow and John Brummer posed for the camera in Westfield before taking a ride on August 21, 1892. Photograph by W. Lachman of Shippensburg; courtesy of the Westfield Historical Society

Cranford Bicycle Club posed before a ride by the Rahway River in 1890. Photograph courtesy of the Cranford Historical Society

Many of the people enjoyed the good life. Here members of the Crescent Avenue Presbyterian Church, Plainfield, show off their Sunday best. Photograph courtesy of the Plainfield Public Library

85

Goat carts were popular. In this instance, John J. Hazler of Elizabeth sat in his cart under the watchful eyes of his young uncles, Augustus and William Wiener, also of Elizabeth. Both cart and goat had to be carried to the photographer's third floor studio. Photograph (circa 1897) courtesy of Alice Elmer

Two young ladies and a gentleman friend found a seat in a two-wheeled farm cart. Photograph (circa 1897) courtesy of the Linden Public Library

A work crew with an ox team worked on a road in Roselle circa 1898. Photograph from a glass slide by John L. Warner; courtesy of William and Ruth Frolich

A work crew was brought to New Orange (Kenilworth) in 1899 to construct 140 houses. Photograph courtesy of the Kenilworth Historical Society

Summer house (gazebo) on the estate of Dr. J. Ackerman Coles in Scotch Plains. Photograph (circa 1876) by Guillermo Thorn; courtesy of the Hatfield family

An unidentified barnyard in Union Township, a familiar scene, date unknown. There are only a few farms left. Photograph courtesy of Ada Brunner

Education began to take the center of the stage in Union County. While some children went to private schools, others attended one-room schools like this one, the Kendall School, New Providence (now Berkeley Heights). This photograph was taken in 1910. Photograph courtesy of Berkeley Heights Historical Society

Children stand in front of the Grant School in 1890. The Grant School in Cranford became the first home of Union College in 1935. After the college moved to its new campus nearby in 1960, the Union County Cerebral Palsy held classes in the school until its building was constructed in Union Township in the 1970s. The building has been razed. Photograph courtesy of the Cranford Historical Society

New Providence School became the New Providence Borough Hall. This photograph was taken by Cornelius Lovell about 1894. Photograph courtesy of the New Providence Historical Society

This mansion was built by A. W. Dimock just before the 1873 stockmarket crash. It became Battin High School in 1889. It was used until June 1912, when a new building replaced it. Photograph courtesy of Elizabeth Public Library

Joseph Battin, president of the Elizabethtown Water Company, gave the Dimock place to the city of Elizabeth to be used as a high school in 1889. Photograph from City of Elizabeth-Illustrated, *1889*

This 1903 view shows the home of Mr. and Mrs. Peter Egenolf on Elizabeth Avenue, which was given to the Elizabeth Day Nursery. The Egenolfs had helped to form the nursery in 1886. It was used until 1977, when the nursery was moved to the former National Cash Register Company building. The nursery, renamed the Egenolf Day Nursery, continues to receive a stipend of $1,000 a month from Egenolf's estate. It cares for about 100 children daily. Photograph courtesy of the Elizabeth Public Library

Peter Egenolf, a German immigrant, served as an aid to Lieutenant General Winfield Scott during the Civil War. He followed General Scott to Elizabeth at war's end and conducted a grocery and tanning business. The depression of 1873 caused him to join the new Prudential Insurance Company as a salesman. He became an executive of the company, serving it for forty years. Photograph from Charles L. Aquilina's collection

Cranford Fire House with the hook and ladder and hose wagons in front, April 1893. Photograph from Louis E. Hendrickson's Cranford, N. J. Illustrated, *1904; courtesy of the Cranford Public Library*

Postmen lined up with their wagons in front of the Rahway Post Office. Photograph (circa 1900) courtesy of the Rahway Historical Society

One of the zaniest races that ever took place in the Arthur Kill was in the 1890s before some 3,000 spectators. The race between two women rowers grew out of a debate between residents of Staten Island and New Jersey over their nautical skills. The race was scheduled to settle the issue. Instead of having men row, two young women were selected. They were Katie Dooley, sixteen, who rowed across the Kill four times a day to work at the Singer plant, and Minnie Mooney, eighteen, a dressmaker, who lived in the "Port."

The hat was passed and fifty dollars was collected for the winner. Because of work hours, the race was held at night. Despite her lack of experience, Minnie crossed the finish line first. Katie's supporters challenged the verdict. Mrs. Thomas Nolan of Staten Island replaced Katie at the oars. Again Minnie won. A party followed the race. According to the Singer Light, there was much absenteeism the next day. Photograph courtesy of the Elizabeth Public Library

David D. Frazee of Westfield was a mason and a veteran of the Civil War. One of his sons was John Henry Frazee. Photograph courtesy of Dorothy Baker

Mary Romelia Stewart of ELizabeth and a child. Mrs. Stewart died on November 8, 1884. Photograph (circa 1880) courtesy of Alice Elmer

Margaret Stewart Day, wife of a Methodist minister, shortly before her death in Elizabeth in 1906. Photograph courtesy of Alice Elmer

William F. Bailey of Summit originated the term "the Hill City" for Summit. It was originally known as Turkey Hill. Photograph courtesy of the Summit Public Library

Reverend Dr. Theodore F. White was pastor of the Central Presbyterian Church, Summit, from 1883 to 1903. He was pastor emeritus of the same church from 1903 to 1910. Photograph (circa 1900) courtesy of the Summit Public Library

In 1889 President Benjamin Harrison, the nation's twenty-third president, visited Elizabeth to commemorate the ceremonial journey taken by President-elect George Washington 100 years earlier. He arrived at the Pennsylvania Railroad Station at 7:23 a.m. on April 29 and was welcomed by Mayor Joseph Grier. Every church bell in the city rang and a twenty-one-gun salute was fired by a group of GAR veterans.

President Harrison had breakfast at the home of Governor Robert Green on Cherry Street. Ceremonies were conducted at the Alcyone Boat Club before the president boarded a barge for the sail across the harbor.

A living arch featuring a young woman on each step, representing each state and territory, was placed across Elizabeth Avenue at the Crossroads (Union Square). The president bowed to the young women as he rode under the arch and was greeted by cheers from the young and the watchers. Photograph from Charles L. Aquilina's collection

The Alcyone Boat Club was decorated for the visit of President Benjamin Harrison. An observer wrote that the float on which the people stood to watch him was so crowded with well-wishers, it was feared that it would sink. Photograph courtesy of Arthur F. Cole

The Cranford Boating Club conducted a successful regatta in 1885. It was so successful that the Cranford Improvement Association invited all residents to participate in the Rahway River Carnival the next year. The festivities were held for two days, July 31 and August 1, 1886. They included canoe, swimming, and double-scull races for ladies. The next day twenty-four boys met at the North Union Avenue dam for the three-mile race downstream to the Williams-Droescher Mill and return.

A band of strolling musicians walked along the river bank playing lively tunes. Chinese lanterns lighted the way. William Sulzer of Roselle, who became governor of New York State, observed that the carnival made him think of Venice. Soon both realtors and the Jersey Central Railroad started calling Cranford the Venice of America or the Venice of New Jersey. Boats were decorated in later carnivals. They are now held occasionally on Nomahegan Lake.

A float in the Cranford River Carnival, 1916. Photograph courtesy of the Cranford Historical Society

The Spirit of St. Louis *was a timely float in 1927, just after Charles Lindbergh's famous solo crossing of the Atlantic Ocean. Harry Heins won a prize for it. Photograph courtesy of the Cranford Historical Society*

Business section of Linden opposite the Wood home. Photograph courtesy of the Linden Public Library

McCormick and Baker store and the Heinz's Keystone delivery wagon on Main Street, Rahway. Photograph courtesy of the Rahway Historical Society

The Charles M. Decker and Brothers store, New Providence Borough. Photograph courtesy of the New Providence Historical Society

Street view in Westfield, 1896. Photograph from Art Work of Union County

J. Augustus Dix, president of the Elizabeth Board of Education, sits in the center with students at the Morrell Street School, Elizabeth, 1885. Photograph courtesy of Howard Wiseman, executive director of the New Jersey Sons of the American Revolution

Class of 1888-89 at Columbian School, Rahway. This photograph was given to the Rahway Historical Society by the Chet Clarke Estate. Photograph courtesy of the Rahway Historical Society

While these children didn't raise the roof at the Linden Public School on East Linden Avenue, they were allowed to climb onto it and to hang out the windows for the photographer. Photograph courtesy of the Linden Public Library

Boys in a Grace Church Sunday School class in Plainfield. Photograph (1889) courtesy of the Plainfield Public Library

A Vanderbilt coach stands on Broad Street near West Grand Street circa 1890. Photograph courtesy of Elizabeth Public Library

John Syers was the driver, Bill Schwartz was the engineer, and George Boehm was the assistant engineer in Rolla 2, an Elizabeth volunteer fire company. Photograph (1885) by A. F. Asnon, Photographers, Elizabeth; courtesy of the Elizabeth Fire Museum

The First Presbyterian Church, Summit, circa 1885, stood in an open field. Photograph courtesy of the Summit Public Library

A funeral hearse in Plainfield, circa 1885. Photograph by Guillermo Thorn; courtesy of the Hatfield family

The Magie house on Magie Avenue, Elizabeth, in the late 1870s. This is now the back of the house. The road was moved to the other side of the dwelling some years later. Photograph courtesy of Marion J. Earl

Broad Street, Elizabeth, 1883. Photograph courtesy of the Elizabeth Public Library

The people in these 1885 photographs are unknown. Photographs from Charles L. Aquilina's collection

The Hazler children—Edward Vincenz, born in 1900; Alice Anna, born in 1904; and John Joseph, born in 1897—were all born in the family home on Broadway near Fourth Street, Elizabeth. Photograph courtesy of Alice A. Elmer

Judge Frederick Adams resided in Summit from 1892 to 1899. Photograph courtesy of the Summit Public Library

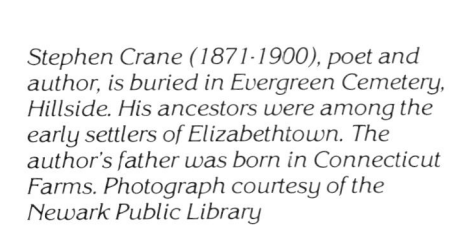

Stephen Crane (1871-1900), poet and author, is buried in Evergreen Cemetery, Hillside. His ancestors were among the early settlers of Elizabethtown. The author's father was born in Connecticut Farms. Photograph courtesy of the Newark Public Library

Children in the Elizabeth Public Schools bilingual program wait to perform at the first Elizabeth Ethnic Festival at the Thomas G. Dunn Sports Center, Elizabeth High School, Elizabeth. Children are taught in their native tongue until they are able to speak English. Photograph by Richard T. Koles

CHAPTER VI
AMERICANS ALL

lizabethtown's early settlers included a varied religious, national and, cultural mix. English settlers were granted the area in 1664 by Governor Nichols after his defeat of the Dutch. Within a year a new governor arrived. Differing attitudes on land title caused the first major clash. Two of the thirty Frenchmen with Governor Philip Carteret were given town lots by him without the original settlers' consent. Fences were torn down, and the court case ended in near riot.

The Dutch recaptured New Amsterdam, and Jacob Melyn, a Dutchman with the original English settlers and John Ogden, Sr., an Englishman, were made *shepens* ("magistrates"). John Ogden, Sr., was also made *schout* ("governor"). Peter Wolverson, a Dutchman, was Elizabethtown's first tavern keeper. A Frenchman, Pierre Jardine, kept an inn at Elizabethtown point as early as 1679.

Jeremiah Peck, the first pastor, strongly opposed church membership for any who had not experienced "true conversion." Reverend Seth Fletcher, the third minister, had trouble with the Quakers. In a letter to Increase Mather in Boston, he wrote: "I have been much molested with Quakers here since I came.... They set themselves to humming, singing, reeling their heads and bodies (antique like) whereby both to disturb me and to take off the people from attending to what I had to say."

Since the First Church meetinghouse was the only church in town, the Quakers must have caused a ruckus in the congregation. Soon new settlers, mostly Scotch Presbyterians, came to the area to escape persecution in England. Entering at Amboy, they went into the wilderness as far as Turkey (New Providence). Although they were preferred to the Quakers, their number gave some concern to the original settlers because they could outvote them in both church and town affairs. The first families included Gordons,

Forbes, Barclays, Fullertons, Crosbys, and "Master Cole," probably the first schoolmaster. The Scotch were industrious and were proud of things religious and familial. They complained about the laziness of the people in Elizabethtown, Piscataway and Woodbridge.

Frank Wiess, a future Elizabethan, posed for the camera in Vienna, Austria, in 1895, shortly before his parents migrated to New Jersey, where his mother became a furrier. Photograph courtesy of Alice Elmer

French Americans

It is fitting, perhaps because the French are usually considered to be romantic, that the first marriage in Elizabethtown was between Daniel Perrin, a Frenchman, and Marie Thorel on February 12, 1665. Nathaniel Bonnel, Elias Boudinot, Francis Barber, and William Trotter were all of French ancestry.

The French Revolution and revolts in the West Indies caused about 120 refugees to seek havens in Elizabethtown. They bought and furnished elegant homes, adding to the currency for area craftsmen and merchants' chests. French fashions, food, furniture, drink, music, art, etiquette, and amusements became the vogue. French manners, such as embracing and kissing upon greeting, were introduced. The elegant lifestyle of the French was a constant fascination for the somewhat staid Presbyterians. Dr. George Ross advertised in both French and English. He was probably the first to use bilingual signs in Elizabethtown, where Spanish signs now abound.

The Americans, who were criticized by the French for drinking, smoking, and failing to keep their servants in their place, soon adopted French styles, attended French language and dancing schools and patronized French dressmakers.

Victor Mercier (seated right) and his family in front of their home in the early 1900s on Kingman Road, New Providence (Berkeley Heights). The Mercier family settled in the "Heights" in the early 1800s. They hoped to raise silk worms and manufacture silk in a mill. They later became farmers and horse breeders. They were among the founders of St. Mary's Roman Catholic Church at Stony Hill and one of the many French families to settle in Union County. Others resided in Elizabeth, Roselle, and Westfield. Photograph courtesy of the Berkeley Heights Historical Society

Afro-Americans

It is unknown when the first Blacks arrived in Elizabethtown. The early settlers in Elizabethtown had servants. Many of these were white indentured persons who worked for a stated number of years to pay for their passage from England. By 1730 Black slaves were listed. The colony's first newspapers carried advertisements for slave auctions and runaway slaves.

Although there was slavery, it was not popular. The Quakers refused to deal with people who owned slaves. Several of the well-known Elizabethans freed their slaves shortly after the Revolutionary War. They included Hannah Ogden, William Livingston, Cavalier Jouet, and Abraham Clark. In 1792 Elias Boudinot initiated the break-up of a ring that was purchasing Blacks in Elizabethtown and reselling them in New Orleans.

Mary Malson Rice, Elizabeth's first Black teacher (center) sits with her family. Others are: (seated left) Sarah Jane Malson and (right) Edward G. Malson; (standing, left to right) Hamilton Clark, Anne Belle Richards Malson, and Totten Smith Malson. Miss Malson taught for fifteen years before becoming a full-time wife and mother. She organized one Brownie and two Girl Scout troops. She was a charter member of the Elizabeth Branch, NAACP, and she was active in St. Augustine's Episcopal Church, Elizabeth. Photograph courtesy of A. Carolyn Rice

Mabel Gertrude Holmes of Elizabeth became both the first Black school principal and, after she retired, the first Black member of the Elizabeth Board of Education. Photograph from Charles L. Aquilina's collection

Kirkpatrick Marrow became the Elizabeth Police Department's first Black detective in the mid-1930s. He later was affiliated with the Essex County Prosecutor's Office. Photograph courtesy of the Elizabeth Police Department

Edward Pierson, bass-baritone, appears with the New York City Opera and in Broadway shows. A native of Chicago's Black ghetto, he now lives in Elizabeth's Elmora section. Photograph courtesy of Mrs. Myrtle Pierson

William M. Ashby, the first Black full-time social worker in New Jersey, formed the Urban League of Union County and served as its director from 1944 to 1953. He is considered to be one of the most outstanding exponents of civil rights in New Jersey. Photograph courtesy of the Newark Public Library

Hand-carved African masks are displayed by (left to right) Steve Sampson and Mary Kinge and Jerome Peterson at the first Elizabeth Ethnic Festival on June 26-28, 1979, at the Thomas G. Dunn Sports Center, Elizabeth High School, Elizabeth. Photograph by Richard T. Koles

Originally the Blacks attended the same churches as the white people. Gradually, small Black churches were formed. The African Methodist Episcopal Ebenezer Church of Rahway was organized in 1826 and is one of the first African Methodist Episcopal churches in New Jersey. It was followed in 1862 by the Bethel Methodist Church on Central Avenue and in 1871 by the Zion Methodist Church on Main Street, both in Rahway. The first Black church in Elizabeth was the Siloam Presbyterian Church, organized in 1867; the earliest in Plainfield was the Mount Olive Baptist Church, in 1870.

The small Black churches provided the Blacks in Union County with leadership and spearheaded education. Oliver Nuttman was placed in charge of a free school for both "colored" children and adults in 1815, after the free school association was formed. The average attendance was sixty-five students. The school must have flourished. On May 11, 1847, a notice was posted stating that "an examination of colored scholars at their schoolroom in East Jersey Street" (Smith, *The School Interests of Elizabeth*) was to be held at two o'clock. Miss Pamela Price was in charge. Thirty-five students met for the examination in a house behind Stephen Pearson's grocery store.

Dr. Joseph E. Brown, a Rahway native and the first Black physician in Union County, was both a church and civic leader. He gave spiritual and financial assistance to others. The Van Deveres, Clifford B. and Arthur, located first in Elizabeth, then in Roselle, became a most dependable source of jobs for Black people as far as Red Bank, where the Van Deveres operated a moving business.

Mary Malson of Elizabeth graduated from the Elizabeth Normal School in 1910 at the top of her class. She was the first Black student to attend the school. The principal recommended that applicants for city teaching posts be selected on the basis of academic standing. There were only seven openings for some dozen students. The board of education agreed. Miss Malson was hired. When it was discovered that she was Black, an outcry arouse to rescind the appointment. The board stood its ground, and Miss Malson became the first Black teacher in the Elizabeth schools. She was soon joined by Miss Mabel Holmes, who became the first Black principal in the county. Miss Holmes, after teaching for forty-two years, also became Elizabeth's first Black school board member. Mrs. Bernice Davis of Linden served as president of the city's first elected board of education. She also was principal of Winfield Scott School 2 in Elizabeth and became director of primary education and executive assistant to the Elizabeth superintendent of schools.

Gradually Blacks began to make their marks in the county. Dr. Charles Lomack, originally of Scotch Plains, became the first Black chairman of the board of managers of the county's hospital, the John F. Runnels Hospital, Berkeley Heights. Everett C. Lattimore, who was Union County's first Black freeholder and freeholder director, became Plainfield's first Black mayor in 1982. He also is the city's assistant superintendent of schools. Herbert Kinch of Rahway became the first Black police chief in the county in 1967.

Union County is known for its excellent Black athletes. Paul Robeson won his initial plaudits as a student at Westfield High School. Captain Marion R. "Ray" Rodgers of Plainfield was a Golden Gloves Champion in 1942 and served as a fighter pilot in World War II. Ron Freeman of Elizabeth was winner of gold and bronze medals in the Olympic Games, and Gil Chapman, an Elizabeth city councilman, was once a pro-football player. Renaldo "Skeets" Nehemiah of Scotch Plains holds the world record in the 100-meter high hurdles.

Blacks are very much a part of the Union County story. From the first, many were trained as artisans. There were many Black shoemakers, blacksmiths, and barbers. By the 1960s, Blacks were represented on many public boards and were assuming positions of importance in business and industry throughout the county. Real estate barriers were disappearing. Their children are being encouraged to complete high school and attend college. In terms of civil rights legislation, Blacks are well past the gate to the promised land, and they are ready to continue sowing its fields, tending the crops, and sharing the harvests. ■

The Irish Americans

The Irish accompanied the early Scots to the New World. Irish names such as William Kelley began appearing as property owners in Elizabethtown as early as 1764.

Most of the Irish migration, however, occurred in the late 1800s. Feelings ran high against these newcomers. The first three Irish families were driven out of Elizabethtown in the 1820s when it was discovered that they were Roman Catholics. Most of the laborers on the Elizabeth and Somerville Railroad, the New Jersey Railroad and Transportation Company, and the Delaware and Lackawanna Railroad were Irish. Soon they also were working in the mills and shops which were situated along the railroads' rights of way.

By 1845 their numbers had increased sufficiently to require churches. Reverend Dr. Nicholas Murray, a native of Ireland and pastor of the First Presbyterian Church in Elizabethtown, spearheaded the transfer of property adjacent to his church's old parsonage to St. Mary's Roman Catholic Church in 1845. St. Mary's Roman Catholic Church was built at Stony Hill (New Providence) in 1847, and St. Mary's Roman Catholic Church in Rahway in 1858.

The Irish formed the nucleus of the new police and fire departments, helped to found hospitals, and began representing their neighborhoods in municipal and county governments. In Elizabeth, Patrick Ryan became the first mayor of Irish extraction. Thomas G. Dunn, the present mayor, is also of Irish descent and holds the record for the longest consecutive service. He has been mayor since 1965.

The increased population created a demand for schools. Elizabethtown and the other communities were faced with the problems of meeting these demands. The Roman Catholic population also formed a parochial school system. One of the first schools was started in 1851 at St. Mary's of the Assumption. A few years later, in 1855, St. Michael's School opened. Both are in Elizabeth.

By the early 1900s John P. Holland, a native of Ireland, had tested and sold a submarine to the United States Navy at Elizabethport, and John W. Whelan had progressed from carpenter to vice-president of the National State Bank, Elizabeth, serving in the latter office from 1912 to 1923.

Ambrose McManus, born in Keighry Head in Elizabeth in 1890, founded McManus Furniture Company on First Street and later built a huge store on East Jersey Street. John S. Connelly, another native of Keighry Head, started the Connelly Street Railway, a horse-drawn trolley that ran between Bond Street, Elizabeth, and Lyon's Farms (now Hillside). ∎

St. Mary's Roman Catholic Church, Elizabeth, 1867. The congregation was primarily Irish. From an old woodcut; courtesy of St. Mary's Roman Catholic Church, Elizabeth, and the Elizabeth Public Library

Reverend Dr. Nicholas Murray, a native of Ireland and pastor of the First Presbyterian Church, Elizabeth, spearheaded the sale of some of the Presbyterian church land to the new St. Mary's parish. Photograph from R. W. Edwin Hatfield's History of Elizabeth

Admiral Alfred Thayer Mahan, U.S. Naval officer and historian, resided at 232 South Broad Street, Elizabeth. He served during the Civil War and was president of the Naval War College at Newport, Rhode Island for two terms. He wrote many works on naval history. His family moved to Elizabeth in 1872. His sister Jane resided in the house for more than seventy years. Photograph courtesy of the Elizabeth Public Library

A black veil was placed on a novice's head at the Benedictine Convent, Elizabeth. This convent serves as the mother house for the Benedictine Sisters, who were primarily Irish or of Irish descent. Photograph from Frank Leslie's Illustrated Newspaper

Henry R. Cannon was first clerk of Union County. He served from 1857 to 1877. Photograph courtesy of Walter G. Halpin

James E. Hennessey of Cranford was the township's police chief for more than twenty-five years. He was appointed in 1901 as the first permanent patrolman. Initially his salary was fifty-five dollars a month. Photograph from A. Van Doren Honeyman's A History of Union County

Dennis Long, a native of Ireland and a farmer in Union Township was active in the development of the borough of Kenilworth and worked as a land purchasing agent for the Rahway Valley Railroad. When he served as president of the Union Township Board of Education, he introduced free books for students. Long Avenue in Hillside, one of the townships' longest streets, is named for him because his farm was on it. Photograph from A. Van Doren Honeyman's A History of Union County

Reverend Thomas B. Larkin was pastor of the St. James' Roman Catholic Church, Springfield. Photograph courtesy of the Newark Public Library

Bender Academy, Elizabeth, 1927. At this time, the school was attended primarily by students of Irish and German descent. Photograph courtesy of Dr. Matthew C. McCue

111

Reverend Edward Stanley, pastor of St. Patrick's Roman Catholic Church, Elizabeth, looked at statue of Reverend Martin Gessner, who founded the parish in 1873. Photograph (1967) courtesy of the Newark Public Library

Mayor Thomas G. Dunn of Elizabeth, elected in 1964, has served in that office longer than any other Elizabeth mayor. He also is a former state senator. He is one of many persons of Irish descent to hold office in Union County. Photograph by Richard T. Koles

Irish participants in the first Elizabeth Ethnic Festival at the Elizabeth High School were Nora Tansev, Bridget Murnane, and Ruth Murnane. Photograph by Richard T. Koles

German-Americans

Wanderlust is a German word. It aptly describes one of the reasons for the Germans' presence in America. The other reason was forced migration due to civil and economic hardships accompanied by military turmoil. In the 1680s William Penn, at one time proprietor of both East and West Jersey, toured the Rhineland offering inducements to the people to migrate. Many of them accepted. The famous Pennsylvania Dutch are from Germany, not Holland.

Most of the Germans joined the hundreds of migrating Irish after the great potato famine swept Europe in 1848. Many were excellent farmers and skilled craftsmen and were quickly assimilated by the communities.

August Ritter, who arrived in Rahway's Fifth Ward (Clark) in 1849, was a successful farmer. His son, August Ritter, Jr., became the township clerk and gained respect for his persistent scrutiny of public accounts.

As the population grew, traffic increased. There were more farm wagons and carriages and new horse trolleys. Protests grew over the traffic jams at the railroad grade crossing. The first railroad bridge was built by Adam Gerloch on the Central Railroad of New Jersey.

The German and Irish population created a demand for beer. Breweries were opened by Carl Eller, who operated Eller's Grove at Elizabeth Avenue near Third Street. With a partner (Eller and Bayer), he operated City Brewery at Pearl Street. Peter Breidt's brewery was a model of productive efficiency. It is said to have been the largest in the state at one time.

One of the fastest rises to municipal power was by Oswald Nitschke, who came to Union County in 1891 and became mayor of Kenilworth in 1919-22, 1928-29 and 1932-33, shortly after becoming a citizen. Oscar, Rudolf, and Edmund Goerke opened a department store in Elizabeth in 1913. They sponsored both the city's business and spiritual development. Edmund became an Elizabeth city councilman.

Carl Schultz was a kind-hearted land developer. In 1884 he donated 400 acres just south of the railroad and funds to build a station on the Delaware and Lackawanna. All he asked in return

August Deinlein, Mrs. Deinlein, and their children and animals on their farm in the early 1900s. The Uzzolino home at 569 Springfield Avenue, Berkeley Heights, is in the background. Photograph courtesy of Berkeley Heights Historical Society

Delicatessen of Henry Wilhelms, Sr., at 803 East Jersey Street, Elizabeth. Photograph courtesy of Dorothy Salter

was that the station be named Murray Hill after the exclusive area in New York City. Charles P. Behre added to the beauty of the already beautiful county by developing one of the largest rose nurseries in the state in New Providence in the late 1890s.

Like the Irish, the Germans too served as police and firemen, became teachers, were employed as skilled workers in growing industrial plants, and operated their own specialized machine shops. It is not uncommon to find several persons by the same name serving a community. In Union Township, for instance, Harold H. Denk was fire chief, while his brother, Jacob F., was police chief. Four Truhes have served the same police department.

The German immigrants brought memories of the *Meistersingers* of the workmen's guilds. Soon, many singing societies were being formed. Although some of them appeared to be German in name, most of them included representatives of all nationalities in the Elizabethport area. The only requirement in most instances was that the man be able to carry a tune, love music and good fellowship, and attend the frequent rehearsals.

Elizabeth pays tribute to the co-operative harmony of representatives of the singing societies. On a granite boulder in Scott Park is enscribed: "Edward Kremser, first prize for City Federation, second class. Won by the United Singers of Elizabeth at Brooklyn, May 29, to June 2, 1915." ■

A bottle opener distributed by the Clauss Bottling Company, Elizabeth. Photograph by Richard T. Koles; from the Charles L. Aquilina collection

The Philip Mohr store and home, where Mohr put ice cream into some seltzer water to make it colder. It became the first ice cream soda. Photograph from City of Elizabeth-Illustrated, *1889*

The Peter Breidt City Brewing Company at 900 Pearl Street was started as the Eller and Bayer Company in 1864. It was purchased by Peter Breidt in 1882 and rebuilt. It was officially closed in January 1920, when the Volstead Act became effective. The site was purchased from the Southern Sash Sales and Supply Company in the early 1970s by the city of Elizabeth for the new Elizabeth High School. Photograph courtesy of the Elizabeth Public Library

The Rising Sun Brewing Company, Elizabeth, was established as the Seeber Brewery Company in 1887 and operated by three generations of Seebers. After it was closed in 1920, it was used as a syrup company, fabrics house, produce warehouse, and bar supply warehouse. Photograph courtesy of the Elizabeth Public Library

Mr. and Mrs. Daniel Mauer of Elizabeth, circa 1900. Photograph courtesy of Alice Elmer

John P. Dengler of Vauxhall Road, Union Township, sat with his family in December 1916. Dengler was the stenographer of the New Jersey Supreme Court, a grower of peaches, pears, apples, and plums, and a breeder of white leghorn poultry. Photograph from A. Van Doren Honeyman's A History of Union County

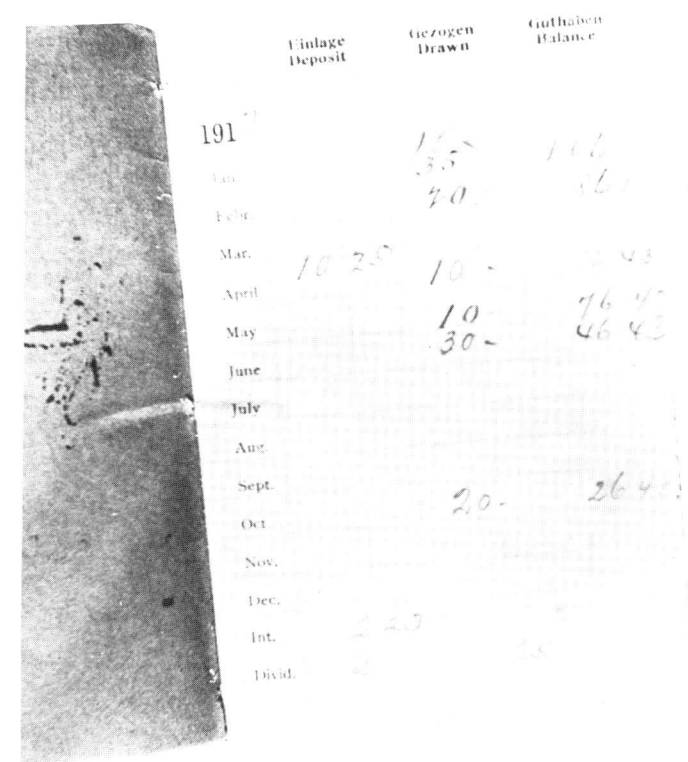

Pass books for the future Harmonia Savings Bank in Elizabeth were in German. Photograph by Richard T. Koles; pass book from Charles L. Aquilina's collection

Edmund Goerke joined the Goerke-Kirch Company, a department store in Elizabeth, in 1913 as a delivery clerk. He soon became secretary and general manager. He served as an Elizabeth city councilman. Photograph from A. Van Doren Honeyman's A History of Union County

Four members of the Truhe family of Union are brother officers. Left to right they are: Deputy Police Chief James Truhe, Retired Police Captain Herbert Truhe, Sr., Police Chief John Truhe, and Deputy Police Chief Herbert Truhe, Jr., all of the Union Police Department. This photograph was taken April 1, 1980. Photograph courtesy of John Truhe

Jewish Americans

While it is believed that Jewish peddlers may have traded with the earliest Dutch and English settlers, the earliest record of a Jewish person in Union County is Lorenzo Da Ponte (1749-1838), a Venetian Jew. He was the librettist for Wolfgang Amadeus Mozart's *Marriage of Figaro, Don Giovanni* and *Cozzi fan Tutte* operas. Unfortunately, his musical skills were unmarketable in Elizabethtown when he arrived about 1805. Like many immigrants after him, he became a vendor, selling tobacco, drugs, and liquors. He stayed in Elizabethtown about a year. Later, he became a professor at Columbia College.

The Naar family, originally Spanish Jews, moved to Elizabethtown from Portugal in 1835. They were farmers, lawyers, and businessmen. David Naar served as an Essex County freeholder in 1842 and mayor of Elizabethtown from 1843 to 1845. He also served in the Court of Common Pleas of Essex County and as consul to St. Thomas from 1845 to 1848.

The German migrations brought the first Jews in large numbers into Elizabethtown. While some were peddlers with packs on their backs, traveling along the hot dusty roads, most were skilled artisans such as tanners, cigar makers, shoemakers, and hatmakers. Some were farmers and shopkeepers. Others started small factories and were laborers and apprentices. The first Jewish congregation, the forerunner of Temple B'nai Israel, met at the home of Mayer Southeimer at 119 Broad Street, Elizabeth, in 1857. The first Jewish cemetery association was Gomel Chesed Hebrew Cemetery Association, formed at the home of Julius Hagin at 410 Magnolia Avenue, Elizabeth, in 1888.

Joseph David migrated from Mannheim, Germany, in 1864 and opened a dry goods store on First Street. His son, Abe, served as a district court judge. The Hersh family migrated to the city in 1866 and started a paper bag business on First Street. Soon they had two stores. The bag business expanded to include groceries and grocery supplies. The business continued to grow. In 1922 Louis F. Hersh erected Elizabeth's tallest building, the Art

Holche Yosher Synagogue, Elizabeth's first Orthodox house of worship, circa 1886. Photograph from Joseph Gale's Eastern Union, The Development of a Jewish Community

Judge David Naar was a mayor of Elizabeth and an Essex County freeholder. Photograph from Joseph Gale's Eastern Union, The Development of a Jewish Community

Decco Hersh Tower. A member of the Union County Trust Company board of directors, he also served as treasurer of the Elizabeth General Hospital.

After 1880 Jews from Poland and Russia began to join the German Jews who were already in Union County. Edward Sachar, a jobber in men's wear in Plainfield, became the father and grandfather of lawyers. Abraham Bardy and Louis Levine operated Bardy's Farms and the now defunct Ideal Dairy, respectively, in Union Township. Bardy's Farms have relocated in Warren Township.

Jewish institutions followed the Jewish population. These included Hebrew free schools, libraries, YM-YWHAs, veterans' posts, B'nai B'rith, Hadassah, the Deborah Tuberculosis League, and welfare groups. The Elizabeth Jewish Free Loan Society, for instance, was started by members of the Gomel Chesed Cemetery Association when John J. Stamler, an attorney, contributed eighty-five-dollars. The amount soon rose to $5,000, and this money was used to help Jews become established.

Jewish leaders such as B. Peter Gold, Bernard L. Goodman, Harry A. Cooper, Harry Weltcheck, Donald Whitken, Abraham Rocker, and Rabbi Gershon B. Chertoff, spiritual leader of the Temple B'nai Israel, are only a few who have contributed much to the county's spiritual, cultural, industrial, and civic growth. ■

From 1885 to 1910, the New Providence (Berkeley Heights) Post Office was located on the porch of this house at 182 Plainfield Avenue. Mrs. Hannah Wahl was the postmistress. It is now part of Vito Mondelli Nurseries. Photograph courtesy of Berkeley Heights Historical Society

Mr. and Mrs. Sam Traubman stood in front of their fruit and vegetable store, Elizabeth, 1912. Photograph courtesy of Florence Traubman

Independent Order Ohwath Zedek completed this building on July 4, 1897. It was also called Library Hall or Charity Hall. Photograph from Joseph Gale's Eastern Union, The Development of a Jewish Community

Portion of the Jewish Education Center, Elizabeth. Photograph by Richard T. Koles

Temple Beth O'r in Clark Township was dedicated in 1966. Photograph courtesy of the Newark Public Library

Temple B'nai Israel, Elizabeth, the first Jewish congregation in Union County, was formed in 1857. Photograph by Richard T. Koles

Rabbi Sally Priesand, the first ordained woman rabbi in the United States, stands in Temple Beth-El, Elizabeth. She was ordained, along with thirty-five men, in 1972 at the Jewish Institute of Religion at Hebrew Union College in Cincinnatti. Prior to coming to Elizabeth in September 1979, she served as associate rabbi two years and assistant rabbi five years at the Stephan Wise Free Synagogue of New York. Photograph by Richard T. Koles

Italian-Americans

Meanwhile, "Little Italys" began to grow in every section of Union County. Nicola Del Nero, a native of Montazzoli, a small farming village high in the Abruzzi Mountains in Chieti Province, Italy, arrived in the Scotch Plains area shortly after the Civil War. He was followed fairly rapidly by others from Montazzoli. By the early 1900s the northern side of Scotch Plains abounded with people with Montazzolese surnames. They formed the San Nicola di Bari Society to honor the saint protecting immigrants. The society offered land and support for building St. Bartholomew Roman Catholic Church, which sponsors an annual festival. Ties between the 5,000 persons of Montazzolian descent, although now in the fifth generation, remain strong. Festival proceedings frequently are sent to the village of Montazzoli.

Thomas Santosalvo, Sr., became the first Montazzolese township committeeman, and Donald Di Francesco became the minority leader of the state assembly in 1982.

West Newark in Hillside and Newark-on-the-Hill in Union Township, real estate developments with eleven-, twelve-, and thirteen-foot lots, were sold to Italian immigrants who thought they were purchasing home sites in the city of Newark.

Superior Court Judge V. William DiBuono of Hillside, assignment judge of Union County, became the first native of Italy to serve on the Hillside Township Committee and to become mayor, municipal magistrate, and director of Union County Civil Defense and Disaster Control. Congressman Matthew J. Rinaldo, a native of Elizabeth, is a child of immigrants.

As in Scotch Plains, many of the Italians, who settled in the New Providence-Berkeley Heights area came from the same village—Benevento near Naples, Italy. Michael Del Duca, one of the first to arrive (1884), worked as a laborer on the railroad and saved money to send for his wife and their five children. Six years after his arrival, he purchased a small farm in Berkeley Heights and conducted a store "where one could buy anything from feed to kerosene (Desmond, *A History of the Township of Berkley Heights*). Nearly 140 persons are descended from Del Duca and his wife.

The section where the Italians lived became known as Peppertown because of the peppers the Italians grew, ate, and sold. Angelo M. Del Duca became one of the first florists in Berkeley Heights. Charles M. Monica became the first mayor of Italian descent in Berkeley Heights in 1947.

In 1901 three young brothers, Louis, Paul, and Carl Vitale, left their native Province of Avalino near Naples to migrate to New Orange Park (Kenilworth). Two years later their parents, Roselle and Sabato, and six brothers and sisters joined them. They established a farm, and the brothers became building contractors. There are more than 250 descendents of these brothers. They have become doctors, policemen, teachers, engineers, and have entered a variety of others careers. They have served on many municipal and county boards.

Joseph Riccitelli moved to Roselle Park after his butcher shop failed in New York City. He bought meat with his remaining ten dollars from a wholesale meat house and sold it door to door. Within six months, he saved enough money to buy a horse and wagon. A rival butcher challenged his business in court. Riccitelli argued his case in court and won. He purchased a store. Later he also entered the building material supply business. Riccitelli became the first marshal in Roselle Park, and he was one of the organizers of the volunteer firemen. He built the borough's first Roman Catholic church.

The Peters brothers in Elizabeth sold their farmland to the new immigrants, whose descendants continue to reside there today. This area along John and Amity streets became known as Peterstown or the Berg. It is considered one of the safest urban neighborhood areas in the state: one can still walk along the street after dark.

One of the best known Italian families in Elizabeth is the La Corte family. Salvatore Francis La Corte was

Joseph Riccitelli of Roselle Park. Photograph from A. Van Doren Honeyman's A History of Union County

Sign for the Ideal Cement Blocks Corporation operated by Joseph Riccitelli. Photograph from A. Van Doren Honeyman's A History of Union County

West Roselle Park Meat Market, Joseph Riccitelli, proprietor. Photograph courtesy of the Roselle Park Historical Society

born in Elizabeth on February 10, 1894, on John Street, where his parents conducted a store. He attended Continental School 3, Battin High School, and Columbia College. In 1916 he received his law degree from Columbia Law School and opened his office at 95 Broad Street. He was appointed a judge. His son, Nicholas J. La Corte, became Elizabeth's first Italian mayor.

Other early Italian families living in Elizabeth who determined the tone of the neighborhood were the Triarsi, Wade, Tavormina, Paternoster, and Corsentino families. The early growth of St. Anthony's parish depended on their dedication.

Their children are results of their community endeavors. Dr. Rocco M. Nittoli was appointed the first president of the board of education in 1949. Anthony Conte became the first Italian-American principal in the Elizabeth public schools in 1956. In 1978 Rocco J. Colelli was appointed the city's first Italian-American superintendent of schools.

George J. Albanese, of Scotch Plains, became Union County's first county manager in 1974 and served until he was named the New Jersey commissioner of Human Services in 1982. Joanne Rajoppi of Springfield has accumulated numerous firsts in her relatively short career. She is the first woman mayor of Springfield and the first Italian chairwoman of the Union County Board of Chosen Freeholders. In 1981 she served as assistant secretary of the state of New Jersey. She also is an editor and author.

Rose Marie Sinnott of Summit (formerly New Providence) became the first Italian woman from those communities to serve as chairman of the Board of Chosen Freeholders. She was a freeholder from 1974 to 1981. She was named Union County surrogate in 1982.

Many other Italian officeholders have been elected and appointed in rapid succession throughout Union County. Nearly 100 years after the first substantial numbers began arriving, the Italians, who had to learn a new language, have taken their place in the land of opportunity. ■

The Church of the Assumption, Roselle Park, replaced an earlier building, now being used as a parish house. Joseph Riccitelli donated the money to build the original church. Photograph by Richard T. Koles

Salvatore F. LaCorte of Elizabeth. Photograph from A. Van Doren Honeyman's A History of Union County

Statue of Christopher Columbus in Scott Park, Elizabeth. Photograph by Richard T. Koles

The Venezia home and country store were built in 1903 on Springfield Avenue in New Providence (Berkeley Heights). James Venezia came to the United States in 1884. He operated a farm. Photograph courtesy of the Berkeley Heights Historical Society

Two firsts: Police Chief Alfred Vardalis and Municipal Judge Anthony Grippo, both of Kenilworth. Grippo also was a surveyor for the New Orange Industrial Association and served as a translator for Italians who were unable to speak English. He later served as mayor. The photograph was taken circa 1921. Photograph courtesy of the Kenilworth Historical Society

St. Anthony's of Padua Roman Catholic Church, Elizabeth, was dedicated on November 6, 1927. The parish was organized in 1895. The church was given its name in 1903, during the pastorate of Reverend Giovanni Bertolotto. When Reverend Leonardo Ruvolo became pastor in 1924, he brought some Salesians of Don Bosco with him. They have provided priests for the church and, since the school opened in 1958, nuns as teachers. Reverend Anthony Bregolato burned the mortage in 1944. Reverend Alvin Menni is the present pastor, and Reverend John F. Murphy is his assistant. Photograph courtesy of Reverend John F. Murphy

The Crestlin Boy's Club, Elizabeth, enjoyed a New Year's Eve party on December 31, 1939, in its clubhouse at Fourth and Amity streets, Elizabeth. Photograph courtesy of Anthony La Qualia

Miss Suzanne Gloria Mauriello (center) of Cranford, new American-Italian Cultural Society Queen for 1979, holds her trophy, flowers, and gifts. With her are (left) Miss Gina Fabbricatore of Newark, 1978 queen, and (right) Miss Josephine Sorce of Elizabeth, 1979 runner up. St. Rocco Festival in Elizabeth. Photograph by Richard T. Koles

Lithuanian-Americans

The first Lithuanians arrived in the early 1870s and found employment at the Singer Sewing Machine Company. Others worked at New Jersey Standard Oil Company and other refineries and in the developing chemical industries in Elizabeth and Linden.

By the mid-1890s there were forty-nine families, enough to form a church. Incorporated as Saints Peter and Paul Roman Catholic Church in Elizabeth, the parish included Newark, Bayonne, and Linden. Reverend Bartholomew Zindzius was the pastor. The number of families continued to increase, and separate parishes were formed in Newark in 1902 and in Bayonne in 1907. Soon the Lithuanians, like the Germans, were organizing language schools, community clubs, choral groups, scouts groups, the Knights of Lithuania, and councils of the Knights of Columbus, and Lithuanians in exile groups.

At one time 14,000 persons in Union County, including 1,000 in Linden alone, listed themselves as Lithuanians. Many of them have become leaders. George Kancierius built an asbestos factory in Linden in 1920. Miss Stephanie Laucius served the Elizabeth school system for forty-five years as teacher, principal, and director of secondary education. Dr. Antomas Bacivicius was the first medical doctor of Lithuanian descent, practicing on Park Place, Elizabeth. Mr. Simon Mack (Mackauskas) opened the first bank in "the port" and served as a general counselor for his neighbors. Dr. William Mack, an Elizabeth mayor, was reputed to be of Lithuanian descent. Another medical doctor, Dr. Joseph J. Butenas, practiced medicine for many years. His home formerly was owned by Miss Arabella Miller, who formed the Pioneer Boys' Club which Butenas attended as a youth.

Dr. Jack J. Stukas, a professor of Seton Hall University, South Orange, formerly of Hillside and Mountainside, conducts a weekly radio program, "Memories of Lithuania," and is a national leader in Lithuanian affairs. ∎

Mayor William Mack, who was also a physician, looks toward Elizabethport. He was said to be a Lithuanian. Photograph by Richard T. Koles

Home and office of Dr. J. J. Butenas at 1037 East Jersey Street, Elizabeth. It is the former home of Arabella Miller. Dr. Butenas is Lithuanian. Photograph by Richard T. Koles

Lithuanian Liepsna Dancers perform at the first Elizabeth Ethnic Festival at the Thomas G. Dunn Sports Center, Elizabeth High School, June 26-28, 1979. Photograph by Richard T. Koles

Polish-Americans

The Polish people's contribution to the style and history of Union County begins with Count Julien Ursyn Niemcewicz, a tutor for young Peter Kean, who was preparing to matriculate to Princeton College. The count became acquainted with Peter's mother, the widow of John Kean. After a brief courtship, they were married.

That he must have been a good husband and admired by his stepson is attested by Peter's naming the family's estate Ursino in his honor. The estate, originally called Liberty Hall, was built by Peter's great-uncle, Governor William Livingston, the New Jersey first governor.

The bulk of Polish migration came 100 years later, when the new arrivals settled in Elizabeth, Linden, Union, and Hillside. They brought with them their institutions. Right Reverend Monsignor Vitus J. Masnicki founded St. Adalbert's Roman Catholic Church in Elizabeth on May 15, 1905, and a parochial school in 1909. The sanctuary was built at Third and Fulton streets, Elizabeth, in 1911. Reverend Joseph A. Smolen continued Reverend Masnicki's work.

Another Polish congregation, St. Hedwig's Roman Catholic Church, was organized in the Bayway section of Elizabeth in 1925, beginning with 350 families. Reverend Venceslau Slawinski was the first pastor. The parish grew rapidly. Before the New Jersey Turnpike and auxiliary highways were built in the 1950s, the church was serving some 960 families. A new church was built in 1960, a convent in 1963, and a school for 300 children a short time later.

The Polish Falcons, a social club for those of Polish extraction, have the slogan, "In a healthy body lies a healthy spirit." Since Nest 126 was chartered in Elizabeth in 1908, Polish groups have contributed to every major activity in Union County. The Falcon's drum and bugle corps has won national recognition.

One of the largest parks in Hillside is named for Police Chief Paul F. Korleski, the township's second police chief. Jacob W. Krowicki, Katherine Green, and Genevieve J. Zagurek, the county's first women constable, have served as grand marshals of annual Pulaski Day parades in New York City.

Joseph J. Leonard became the first Polish councilman in Union County

Count Julian Ursyn Niemcewicz, second husband of Susan Livingston, was a Polish patriot. Photograph courtesy of Mrs. John Kean

Susan Livingston, a niece of Governor William Livingston, married the first John Kean. After his death, she became the wife of Count Julian Ursyn Niemcewicz. Photograph courtesy of Mrs. John Kean

Youngest members of the Konopka Dance Ensemble perform at the Polish Festival in Warinanco Park, Roselle, June 26, 1977. Photograph courtesy of New Jersey Newsphotos, Inc.

when he represented Elizabeth's old First Ward from 1938 to 1949. Edward J. Murawski became the first Polish city council president in Linden, serving from 1967 until his death in 1979. Edward Horbacz became Garwood's first Polish mayor in 1975. John Soja of Elizabeth, named magistrate in 1965, is the first Polish-American municipal judge in Elizabeth and has the longest active record. Walter M. Ceglowski of Hillside, the magistrate in 1934, also served as the school board's attorney from 1941 to 1947.

Raymond Lesniak became the first Polish state assemblyman from Union County in 1977, and freeholder Blanche Banasiak became the first Polish-American chairman of that board in 1982. Freeholder Edward J. Slomkowski, a traffic safety officer with the Union Township Police Department, wrote *Adolescent Attitudes Toward the Police.*

The Polish contributions to Union County are substantial. ■

Two-year old Jennifer Paszkowski wore a native dress called a krakowianka as did the doll behind her at the first Elizabeth Ethnic Festival at the Thomas G. Dunn Sports Center at the Elizabeth High School, Elizabeth. Jennifer was one of the hundreds of people in native costume who participated in the festival. Photograph by Richard T. Koles

Halina Hercek, eight years old, of Scotch Plains was picked up by New Jersey Governor Brendan Byrne after he signed a proclamation commemorating the union movement in Poland on February 19, 1981. Thomas Cukier, also eight years old, watches. The children are dressed in Polish costumes. They accompanied the members of the Polish Culture Foundation of New Jersey. The proclamation praised the Solidarity movement in Poland. Photograph courtesy of the New Jersey Newsphotos, Inc.

Portuguese-Americans

One of the quietest and least noticed migration has been by the Portuguese, who have come to Union County from Portugal and the Canary Islands. By March 18, 1922, there were enough men to form a social club, the Portuguese Instructive Social Club, Inc. Three years later, Joao P. Guerreiro, the first president, spearheaded construction of a social hall. The story of the financing of the American Hall, the focal point of the Portuguese society, gives a true picture of both the interest in education and the seriousness of the Portuguese's belief in their heritage and in America's future. The $250,000 debt was paid off within seven years. It was financed by members' pledges, not a bank loan.

The largest Portuguese influx into Union County came after World War II and rivals Newark in size and importance. As in Newark, the Portuguese operate a wide variety of small shops, mostly in the Elizabethport area, and are contractors and manufacturers.

Our Lady of Fatima Roman Catholic Church at 601-607 First Street, organized in 1973, serves the spiritual needs of more than 10,000 Portuguese communicants. Reverend John S. Antao, the pastor, has gained statewide recognition for his work among senior citizens.

Although politically aware, the Portuguese leaders, from Joao P. Guerreiro to Paulo Fonseca, the present president of the Portuguese Instructive Social Club, have stressed cooperation rather than protest. ∎

Performing a Portuguese dance in costume at the Dunn Sports Center, Elizabeth High School, Elizabeth, were (left to right) Lucy Rodrigues and her brother, Manuel, Eugenia Esteves, all of Union Township, and Ferando Vieira of Elizabeth. Photograph courtesy of New Jersey Newsphotos, Inc.

Cuban-Americans

Edward Stratemayer, a famous Elizabeth author, published the Tom Swift and Rover Boys series. He modeled his heroes on the success format of Horatio Alger, Jr. Were he alive during the Cuban migration, he would have included many of them as examples.

The story of the Cuban migration is unlike any other in the county's history. Cuban exiles since Fidel Castro's takeover in 1959 have had unprecedented success in merging into the mainstream of economic, political, and civic life in Elizabeth and surrounding communities.

Except for the early French refugees, it has taken most groups at least two generations to achieve social, economic, and civic status. The Cubans have become businessmen, professors—such as Dr. Orlando Edreira, chairman of the Foreign Language Department at Kean College—and home owners. They also have contributed greatly to the social and educational climate in Union County. This has been done by renovating old buildings, opening restaurants and stores, and transforming run-down streets for the revitalization of the Elizabethport area.

Raphael Fajardo, Jr., appointed by President Ronald Reagan as an observer to the San Salvador election in 1982, is also on the Elizabeth Board of Education, following Carlos Ferrer, the first Hispanic member. Louis Bargas has been president of the Cuban Board of Trade since 1980. Samuel Rodriguez, an early leader in the Elizabeth Cuban community, is the first Hispanic-American councilman of Elizabeth.

In Elizabeth, where the majority of the Cubans live, there are twenty clubs and associations. Two Spanish-language newspapers keep the community informed. A telephone directory is published in Spanish. A literary magazine is anticipated by 1982.

The motto, *Una Nueva Vida* ("a new life"), though Spanish, could be the motto for countless others who have come to America's shores. The Cubans have brought it up to date. ∎

A bust of Cuban patriot Jose Marti was placed in Elizabeth Park in 1966. Photograph by Richard T. Koles

A crowd gathers on April 15, 1980, in Elizabethport for a prayer before Cuban march for solidarity through Elizabeth. Photograph courtesy of the New Jersey Newsphotos, Inc.

American—Every One

One of the most exotic groups to arrive in the mid nineteenth century were the gypsies, who camped for many years in the Vauxhall section of Union Township and on Great Island on the Elizabeth-Newark line. They arrived each spring, told fortunes and traded horses, and departed each fall. There were three major groups: English, Spanish, and Hungarians. Gypsy funerals, in which the queens and kings were buried in Rosedale Memorial Park in Linden and Evergreen Cemetery in Hillside, were observed with curiosity.

While many nationality groups moved into Elizabethport in the footsteps of the earlier settlers, others built small enclaves in various communities. There were Serbs in Elizabeth, some fifty Hungarians in Hillside in 1918 and, ten families of Ukrainians in Plainfield by 1936. A section along Centennial Avenue in Cranford is known as Turkeytown because of the number of refugees, mostly Armenians, from the Ottoman Empire.

Each of these groups has gradually taken its place in the county. The Ukrainians, for instance, proudly point out that two of their heritage, William Gural of Springfield and Noel Musial of Scotch Plains, have served as mayors of Hillside and Scotch Plains, respectively. ∎

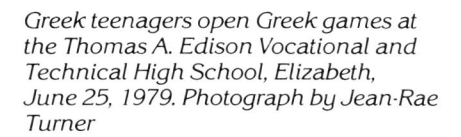

Puerto Rican display at the first Elizabeth Ethnic Festival. Photograph by Richard T. Koles

Greek teenagers open Greek games at the Thomas A. Edison Vocational and Technical High School, Elizabeth, June 25, 1979. Photograph by Jean-Rae Turner

Irene Lewycky (left) and Helen Fedun exhibit Ukrainian art objects at the first Elizabeth Ethnic Festival. Photograph by Richard T. Koles

Enjoying some food at a Greek festival at the Holy Trinity Greek Orthodox Church, Westfield, circa 1977, are (left to right) Theo Kiriakatis of Kenilworth and Steve Horner of Cranford. Theo is dressed in a sixty-year-old, hand-made costume from Theves, Greece, and Steve is dressed as an Euzone, a soldier in the Greek war for independence in the 1820s. Photograph courtesy of New Jersey Newsphotos, Inc.

Mr. and Mrs. Bela B. Lukacs of Murray Hill pick up their seating cards at the nineteenth annual carousel ball for the benefit of the American Hungarian Foundation at Fiddlers Elbow Country Club, Bedminster. (Murray Hill is part of New Providence.) Mr. Lukacs is treasurer and director of the American Hungarian Foundation and a Hungarian leader in Union County. Photograph courtesy of New Jersey Newsphotos, Inc.

The neighbors gather on a porch in Fanwood circa 1900. Photograph courtesy of the Fanwood Memorial Library

Relatives of the Day family stopped to have their photographs taken at the Murray Hill railroad station when they came to a family reunion circa 1900. Photograph courtesy of Berkeley Heights Historical Society

View of Engine Company No. 2, Elizabeth, circa 1900s. Photograph from a postcard by the Elizabeth Novelty Company; courtesy of the Elizabeth Fire Museum

CHAPTER VII
1900 – Present
INTO THE TWENTY-FIRST CENTURY

The year 1982 marks the 125th anniversary of the formation of Union County. In those years, the county has changed from a rural society of seven small farm and business-oriented communities to a bustling urban-suburban area in the heart of metropolitan New York.

According to the United States Bureau of the Census, the per capita income of the people in Union County's twenty-one municipalities is 33 percent above the national average. This means that the people in the county's five cities, eight townships, seven boroughs, and one town rank among the highest paid in the nation.

Since Edison's successful experiments, Holland's submarines, and Marconi's wireless, many individuals and firms have found better and more effective ways to produce consumer goods through research and development. The Bristol-Myers Company, Hillside; Schering-Plough Corporation, Union and Kenilworth; Merck and Company, Rahway; Ciba-Geigy Corporation and Celanese Corporation, both Summit; and the Exxon Research and Development Company, Linden, are among these.

The Singer Company introduced methods of mass production that continue to be used in assembly lines throughout the county. The county, with 1,500 industries, is a leader in the petrochemical industry. Many of these industries are nationally-known concerns like General Motors Corporation in Linden, Mack Truck Corporation in Hillside, and Burry-Lu Corporation in Elizabeth.

Others like E. L. Ewertsen and Sons, Inc. in Kenilworth, which made parts for the initial Telestar satellite, are small specialists. The companies account for 175,000 employees. The county ranks second in the state in

Michael Hennessy (center) sits with his class in the New Orange School (McKinley School). The school was under the jurisdiction of Cranford until Kenilworth was formed. This photograph was taken in 1902.

Mamie Stein, the small girl at the extreme right, was killed in the American Can Company explosion in Kenilworth sixteen years later. The company made gunpowder for the Russian army during the Russian Revolution. After the United States entered World War I, it made gunpowder for the American forces. Some people suspected the company was sabotaged. Six other persons were killed. Photograph courtesy of the Kenilworth Historical Society

133

manufacturing payroll and capital expenditures for manufacturing.

As it was during the Revolutionary War, the county continues to be at the hub of transportation. The automobile, as the railroad and trolley car did earlier, opened up remote areas after World War I. Meadows became residential subdivisions. Among the earliest were Townley and Larchmont in Union Township, Wychwood in Westfield, and Sleepy Hollow in Plainfield. Many others followed.

U.S. Route 1, the nation's oldest highway, bisects the county. It has been joined by the Lincoln Highway (Route 27); the old Morris Turnpike (Routes 24 and 82); Routes 28 (the Old York Road), 22, and 78; the New Jersey Turnpike (Route 95); and the Garden State Parkway. They place the county within four hours of Washington, D.C., five hours of Boston, Massachusetts, and a half-hour of New York City.

The air age came to Union County in October 1917, when the Standard Aircraft Corporation announced that it would produce sixty planes a week at its building in Elizabeth. Langley Field, a small airstrip, was built for test flights. The initial planes were unsatisfactory. In October 1919 the machinery was sold at auction. There also was an airfield in Westfield and an emergency landing strip in Kenilworth.

In 1928 the city of Newark opened the Newark Airport, which has advanced steadily into the city of Elizabeth. Nearly half of the Newark International Airport's facilities are in Union County. The terminals are within a ten-minute drive from the Union County Courthouse. The world is just a jet away from Union County.

The Linden Airport was started during World War II to transport airplanes built in the city to the war zones. Linden leases the airport to a private contractor who operates the airport. The New Jersey Civil Air Patrol is based at the port.

Since 1962, when Sea Land introduced the container ship, Elizabeth has become one of the major container ship ports in the world. The Port Authority of New York and New Jersey also operates major port facilities in Elizabeth and operates the airport. The highways, railroads, seaport, and airport have all caused Union County to become a center for warehousing and distribution.

Although Elizabethtown lost Princeton University and Kenilworth lost Upsala College, Union County may boast two institutions of higher learning: Kean College of New Jersey (originally Newark State College), which moved to Union Township in 1958, and Union College, a two-year college in Cranford, formed in 1935. It also has the Union County Vocational and Technical School, now a part of Union County College, and numerous private technical and business schools.

Most of the communities have historical societies which are preserving early dwellings. There are many dramatic groups and several musical groups which bring plays and concerts to the public on a regular basis. The New Jersey and Garden State ballet companies make regular appearances. The Summit Art Center and the college galleries feature year-round exhibits, while Clark, Plainfield, Kenilworth, and Union and several of the temples and churches conduct annual shows. Ethnic festivals are featured annually in Warinanco Park in Roselle.

The county's population grew from an estimated 25,000 in 1857 to an estimated 504,100 in 1982. Union County contains representatives of nearly every nationality and racial, religious, and occupational group in the world. As they did with the early Scotch and French refugees, the people continue to open their hearts, homes, and pocketbooks to refugees from foreign lands—Russian Jews from the USSR, Cubans, Haitians, and Vietnamese, just to mention a few. In addition, the county's residents, individually and through their agencies, are among the first to provide relief for Italian earthquake victims, hungry works in Poland, and homeless Cambodians.

Although the county is heavily industrial, there are fine residential sections in every community, and some—like Mountainside, Fanwood, Scotch Plains, Summit, Berkeley Heights, New Providence, and Westfield—are known as "bedroom communities," which offer fine suburban living for persons employed in New York City, Newark, Elizabeth, or Trenton.

"Union County has it all," former freeholder John K. Meeker, Jr., when 1982 chairman of the Board of Freeholders declared. "As we celebrate its 125th anniversary, we are celebrating the county's past and what we feel will be a bright and prosperous future."

Union County is a precious jewel still undiscovered by many. ∎

Rahway Gun Club, May 28, 1904. This photograph was given to the Rahway Historical Society by the Chet Clark Estate in 1975. Photograph courtesy of the Rahway Historical Society

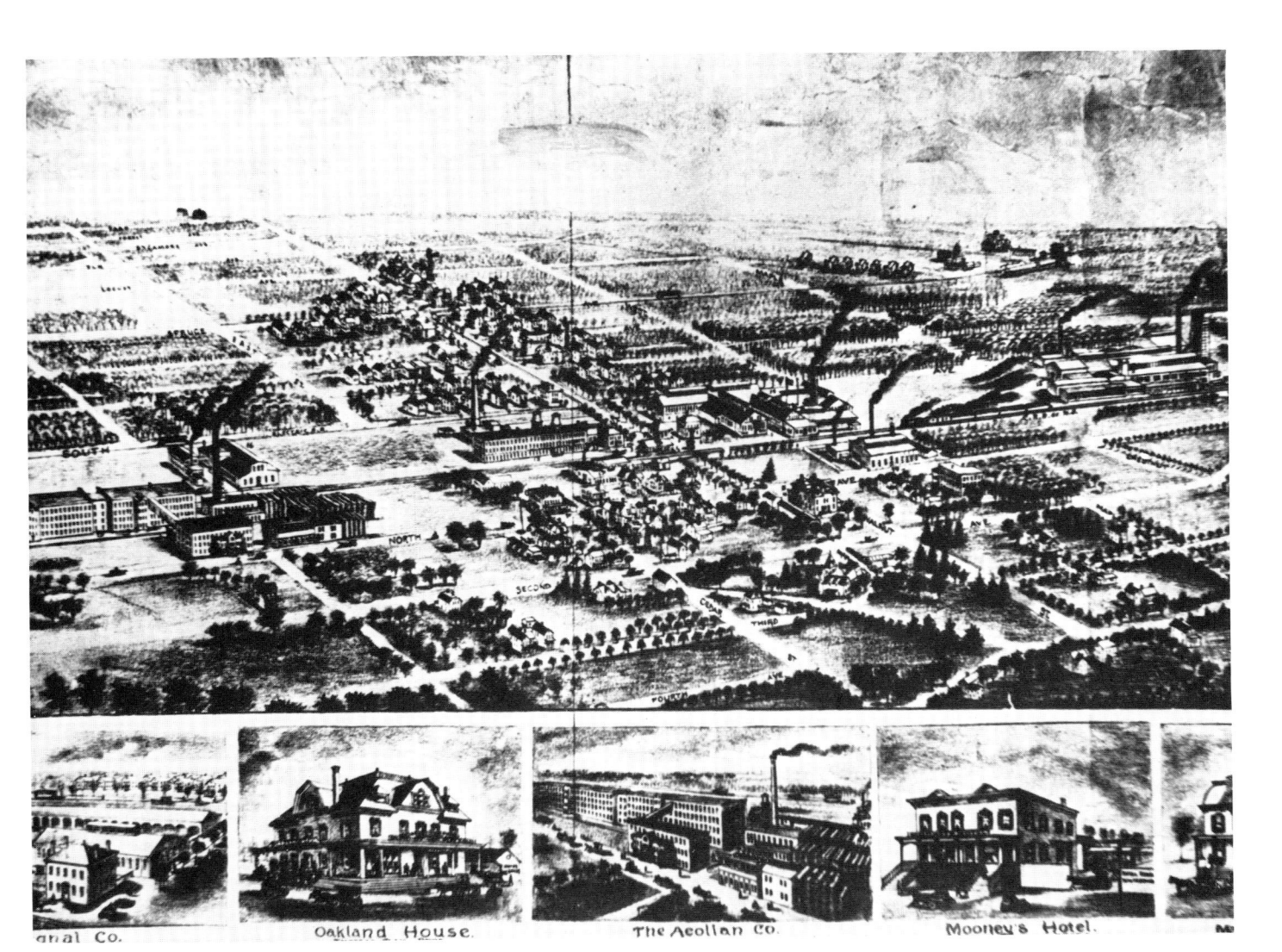

A 1903 view of Garwood shows the streets, factories, and small illustrations of the Hill Signal Company, the Oakland House, the Aeolian Company, and Mooney's Hotel. Photograph courtesy of the Newark Public Library

This open-air trolley on Broad Street, Elizabeth, had a cow catcher on the front of it. The Arch was in the background. Photograph courtesy of the Cranford Historical Society

Trolley on Elm Street, Westfield, 1907. Photograph courtesy of the Westfield Historical Society

Alice Lakey of Cranford was responsible for the first federal Pure Food Drug Law in 1906. Photograph courtesy of the Cranford Historical Society

Trolley car passed through the Arch in Elizabeth against traffic circa 1920s. Photograph from the Fiftieth Anniversary Booklet of the Division 823, Amalgamated Transit Union, 1968; courtesy of the Roselle Public Library

Elizabeth Frazee of Westfield and her cousin, Mildred Frazee, also of Westfield, about 1905. Photograph by Kern's Theatrical Coping House, New York City; courtesy of Dorothy Baker

The YMCA movement swept through Union County in the 1890s. By the 1900s there were Y's in Plainfield, Rahway, Westfield, Summit, and Elizabeth, providing residential facilities and recreational activities for young men.

The Plainfield YMCA. Postcard courtesy of the Plainfield Public Library

The Elizabeth YMCA conducted shop meetings beside a railroad siding. Note the organist and portable organ at the right. This circa 1900 meeting must have been a Sunday religious service. Photograph courtesy of Kathleen Dunn, YMCA of eastern Union County

Drawing of the Elizabeth YMCA which replaced an earlier storefront. Photograph (circa 1904) courtesy of Kathleen Dunn, YMCA of Eastern Union County

Boys play in the boys' department of the Elizabeth YMCA, 1907-1908, in the new building on East Jersey Street near Broad Street. Photograph courtesy of Kathleen Dunn, YMCA of Eastern Union County

Anne Wiener Hazler and her daughter, Alica Anna, in Elizabeth, 1907. Photograph courtesy of Alice A. Elmer

When the New Orange Industrial Corporation learned that the fledgling Swedish Upsala College, then in Brooklyn, New York, was looking for a site, it offered a fourteen-acre plot in New Orange. The college, founded in 1893, moved to New Orange (Kenilworth) in the fall of 1898. The college used the nearby fields for football and baseball. The Kenilworth location was a disappointment to the college. In 1924 the college relocated in East Orange. The hill where Old Main stood was leveled, and houses were built. The area became Blackburn Park in 1950.

Upsala College faculty at New Orange (Kenilworth) in 1905. Photograph courtesy of Upsala College Library

View of the Upsala College campus, Kenilworth, circa 1900. Photograph by J. Fieldman; courtesy of the Upsala College Library

This rear view of Old Main shows barn and pond. The area was known as Viking Field because many of the students at Upsala were Swedish. Photograph (circa 1900) courtesy of the Upsala College Library

Baseball was the first intercollegiate sport started at Upsala College in 1904. Photograph by W. Hoffer, New York City; courtesy of the Upsala College Library

Gymnasts at Upsala College, Kenilworth, 1913. Photograph by J. Fieldman; courtesy of Upsala College Library

The president's house at Upsala College, New Orange (Kenilworth). Note the boardwalks in front of the fence. Boards were used prior to cement because the dirt paths became too muddy. In Linden, people took the boards up at night to protect them from thieves. Photograph courtesy of the Upsala College Library

Upsala College tennis team, date unknown. Photograph courtesy of the Upsala College Library

The tiny building at the right was used as a chapel for Upsala College (Kenilworth) from 1897 to 1899. It later served as the community's post office and jail. This photograph was taken circa 1913 during a volunteer firemen's block dance. Photograph courtesy of the Upsala College Library

Class of 1921, Upsala College. Photograph courtesy of the Upsala College Library

143

This view of Brunswick Avenue, Elizabeth, shows refinery construction, May 25, 1908. Photograph courtesy of Exxon Corporation

By 1907 representatives of the new Standard Oil Company of New Jersey had purchased farms along Morss's Creek in Linden and in Bayway, Elizabeth, for a refinery that would cover 1,500 acres. Construction started the same year. The first still began operation in 1909. The Bayway Refinery and Bayway Chemical Plant of Exxon Company, U.S.A., and Exxon Chemical Americas, subsidiaries of Exxon Corporation, operate together at the site.

The companies receive crude oil by tanker from all around the world and refine and process the raw materials to produce millions of gallons of gasoline, jet fuel, heating oil, and petrochemical products daily.

Laying of the cornerstone at Machine Shop No. 2 at the Standard Oil Company of New Jersey on January 18, 1908. Photograph courtesy of the Exxon Corporation

Batch stills were put into operation at the Standard Oil Company of New Jersey in 1909. Note the open freight cars carrying coke. Photograph courtesy of the Exxon Corporation

The first locomotive arrived at the new Standard Oil Company of New Jersey refinery on April 13, 1908. It was greeted by Oscar De Hart (standing lower right in white shirt), who was the original engineer in the construction of the refinery. Photograph courtesy of the Exxon Corporation

New factories and new houses created a demand for more trolley lines. This work crew is installing rails in Roselle Park circa 1900. Photograph courtesy of the Roselle Park Historical Society

The Regina Music Box Company, founded in 1892 by Gustave Adolph Brachhausen in Jersey City, moved to Rahway in 1896. The music boxes gained instant popularity. Photograph from Art Work of Union County, *1896*

These handsome phonographs were made by the company in the 1920s. The company now manufactures the electric broom. Photograph courtesy of the Newark Public Library

Hospital cases were sent to Newark until 1877, when the Muhlenberg Hospital was opened in Plainfield. Other hospitals followed in rapid succession. There are now ten hospitals in the county. This is Elizabeth General Hospital and Blake Memorial, Elizabeth, organized in 1879. Photograph courtesy of the Elizabeth Public Library

These young men gathered at the curb to inspect a new car (circa 1910). Tuthill's Hardware Store on Chestnut Street, Roselle Park, was behind them. Note the lawn mowers lined up in front of store. Photograph courtesy of the Roselle Park Historical Society

The McKinley School, New Orange (Kenilworth), about 1902. From Louie E. Henderickson's Cranford, N. J. Illustrated; *courtesy of the Cranford Public Library*

Miss Inez Jessup, the first kindergarten teacher in New Providence, with her class about 1909. Photograph courtesy of the New Providence Historical Society

The Roll family of Linden in 1909. Photograph courtesy of the Linden Public Library

Plainfield Fire Department, circa 1900s. Photograph courtesy of the Plainfield Public Library

Fireman Isaac Van Pelt of Elizabeth. Photograph courtesy of the Elizabeth Fire Museum

Plainfield silver hose cart carriage, June 18, 1909. Photograph courtesy of the Newark Public Library

This interior view of Engine Company No. 2, Truck company No. 4, in Elizabeth shows old brass beds and men playing cards. Photograph courtesy of the Elizabeth Fire Museum

This photograph of the fire department in Roselle Park included the company's dog. Photograph (1907-08) by T. C. Knight; courtesy of the Roselle Park Historical Society

It took earthmoving equipment three years (1903-06) to move Tin Kettle Hill in New Orange (Kenilworth) so it could be used as fill for the Pennsylvania Railroad. The hill is believed to have been used as the site of one of the Revolutionary War beacons because many cannonballs were found by the diggers. They are believed to have been fired during the Revolutionary battles in June 1780. Photograph courtesy of the Kenilworth Historical Society

Two idealistic colonies were started in Union County before World War I. Andress Floyd of Union Township started the Selfmaster Colony, which flourished for twenty-one years; and Bolton Hall spearheaded the formation of Free Acres in New Providence Township, now Berkeley Heights.

Laying granite blocks on Cherry Street, Elizabeth. Photograph courtesy of Reverend William F. Kelly

Andress S. Floyd and his wife Lillian started the Selfmaster Colony to rehabilitate male alcoholics. In addition to housing and feeding the men, the Floyds conducted weaving and printing work programs. The alcoholics wove silk and cotten rugs and table cloths and printed booklets. They also worked for nearby farmers. The Floyds closed the colony after Andress lost large amounts of the money in 1929. Photograph from Andress Floyd's The Making Of Our Books

The Girl Scout House in Friberger Park, Union Township, is all that remains of the Selfmaster Colony. Photograph by Richard T. Koles

Bolton Hall provided his sixty-acre farm for Free Acres after he read and agreed with Henry George, Jr.'s single tax theory in 1910. The colony was one of several experimental colonies started at the time. The land belonged to the community. Individuals paid rent for their portions. The Free Acres Association, Inc. in turn paid the required taxes to New Providence Township, now Berkeley Heights. Photograph courtesy of Berkeley Heights Historical Society

Originally summer cottages like this one were placed on the land at Free Acres. Each member of the Free Acres folk had a half acre. Each person was a member of the governing body. At first it was a summer colony. The community attracted many talented people: William Crawford, an artist; Konrad Bercovici, who composed the Volga Boatman; *MacKinley Kanter, author of* The Best Years of Our Lives; *Victor Killian, an actor; and Thorne Smith, who wrote* Topper. *James Cagney, the actor, was among the famous visitors to the colony. As major highways were built, many residents turned their summer homes into year-round dwellings. Photograph courtesy of New Jersey Newsphotos, Inc.*

Worthington Whittredge, an artist, had his studio at his home at 166 Summit Avenue. He was known as a landscape painter of the Hudson River School. Photograph courtesy of the Summit Public Library

Mrs. Roland D. V. Parker read in her home in New Providence Township, now Berkeley Heights, in the early 1900s. Her husband was township clerk from 1900 to 1903. Photograph courtesy of Berkeley Heights Historical Society

Charles C. Boyd was mayor of Kenilworth from 1907 to 1909 and from 1916 to 1918. Photograph courtesy of the Kenilworth Historical Society

"Aunt" Carrie Bettman, a teacher in the Scotch Plains School, became the first postmistress of Fanwood. She served from 1897 to 1921 in this little office. Photograph from a postcard; courtesy of the Roselle Public Library

Children in the Hillside School, Union Township (Hillside Avenue School, now Walter O. Krumbiegel School, Hillside) did exercises circa 1900. Photograph courtesy of Howard J. Bloy

Children line up in front of the Diamond Hill School in the early 1900s in New Providence, now Berkeley Heights. The hill was so named because of sparkling quartz stones found in the area. The one-room school, the last one to be used in Union County, was closed in 1934. It is now the home of Dr. and Mrs. (Vera) Walter Paist. Photograph courtesy of Berkeley Heights Historical Society

A girls' classroom in Plainfield High School, 1910. Photograph courtesy of the Plainfield Public Library

Louise Connolly served as superintendent of schools of Summit from 1906 to 1910, a time when few women rose to such lofty posts. Photograph courtesy of the Summit Public Library

Children sit at attention in the Linden Public School on East Linden Avenue near Ward Avenue, Linden. Photograph courtesy of the Linden Public Library

This small building was used as a school in Union Township for more than 100 years. Photograph from a postcard (circa 1910); courtesy of the Union Township Police Department

The Rahway River, Cranford. The old mill is in the rear at the left. Photograph from Souvenir Program, Cranford Carnival, July 4, 1916; courtesy of Robert J. Fridlington

The Chancellor, a sidewheeler, carried train passengers from the Elizabeth terminal to Liberty Street, New York City. Photograph courtesy of the Elizabeth Public Library

New Jersey Dry Dock Company and Staten Island Ferry at Elizabethport. Photograph courtesy of the Elizabeth Public Library

The freight steamer Meta was operated by the New York and New Jersey Steamboat Company in 1900. By 1913, when the industrial exposition was held in Elizabeth, the Meta was out of service. The trip from Elizabeth to New York took an hour and a quarter. Photograph courtesy of the New Jersey Historical Society

Riker Electric Vehicle Company, Elizabethport, in 1899-1900. Photograph courtesy of the New Jersey Historical Society

Postcard view of the Elizabeth railroad stations in 1906. Postcard courtesy of John Doyle

Mrs. Charles Waite and her son Robert looked at an early tractor at the Aldene Freight Station in 1910. Photograph courtesy of the Roselle Park Historical Society

The Great Atlantic and Pacific Tea Company at 91 Broad Street, Elizabeth. Photograph from City of Elizabeth-Illustrated, *1889*

C. C Pierson was a carpenter and builder in Elizabeth. Photograph from City of Elizabeth-Illustrated, *1889*

The Drake Opera House, Elizabeth, was one of several theaters in Union County where vaudeville shows were presented. Photograph courtesy of the Elizabeth Public Library

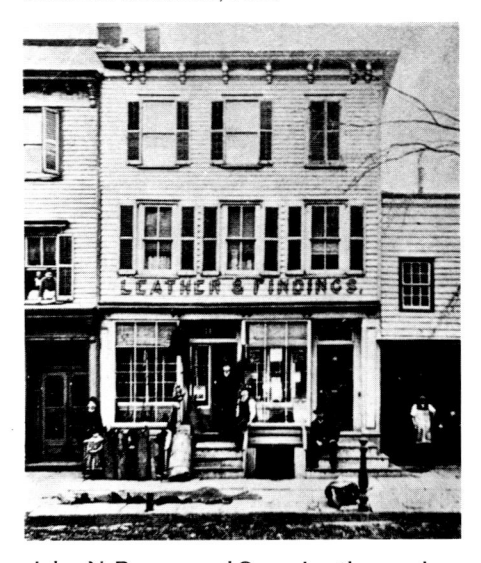

John N. Burger and Sons, Leather and Shoe Findings, were located at 1172 Elizabeth Avenue, Elizabeth. Photograph from City of Elizabeth-Illustrated, *1889*

Broad Street and East Jersey Street looking toward the Arch, Elizabeth, circa 1900. Photograph courtesy of the Elizabeth Public Library

Cast of the Roselle High School senior play in 1909. Photograph courtesy of William and Ruth Frolich

School One in Scotch Plains was designed by Stanford White, the famous architect. It is now vacant. Postcard from Charles L. Aquilina's collection

The Westfield band in 1912. Photograph courtesy of the Westfield Historical Society

Five little boys pulled a flower-decorated carriage containing a single girl as the fiftieth entry in a 1916 parade in Cranford. Photograph courtesy of the Cranford Historical Society

This party at the home of Rebecca Elmer in Cranford in 1914 must have turned into a howling success. Photograph courtesy of the Cranford Historical Society

"And if elected I promise to..." President William Howard Taft, Republican candidate, as he appeared in Westfield in May 1912. Photograph courtesy of the Westfield Historical Society

President William Howard Taft campaigned in 1912 in front of Munoz's house, Alden Street, Cranford. Theodore Roosevelt, the independent candidate, appeared in Union County the same week. Photograph courtesy of the Cranford Historical Society

The post office in Murray Hill in 1912 was located just north of the railroad. Photo shows (left to right) Ruth and Esther Alpaugh, Dorothy Badgley, and Margaret Adams. Photograph courtesy of Berkeley Heights Historical Society

The John T. Kanane Building in Kenilworth was built in 1899. Kanane served as postmaster from 1905 to 1912. He also was deputy sheriff of Union County. His daughter Mary became a surrogate of Union County and a Union County freeholder. This photograph was taken about 1912. Photograph courtesy of the Kenilworth Historical Society

Ernestine Keller rides in a pony cart on Hillside Avenue, Hillside, near Hillside School, now Walter O. Krumbiegel School. Cliff Doremus is driving the cart. The photograph was taken during a Fourth of July parade in either 1916 or 1917. Photograph courtesy of Kathryn Keller

The former John Drew estate in Mountainside was purchased in 1896 by the Children's Country Home and converted to a home for crippled children. The first child was accepted in 1897. It's now the Children's Specialized Hospital, New Providence Road, Mountainside.

The original entrance and wing, added in 1910. Photograph courtesy of the Newark Public Library

Fresh-air sleeping quarters at the Children's Country Home. Photograph courtesy of the Newark Public Library

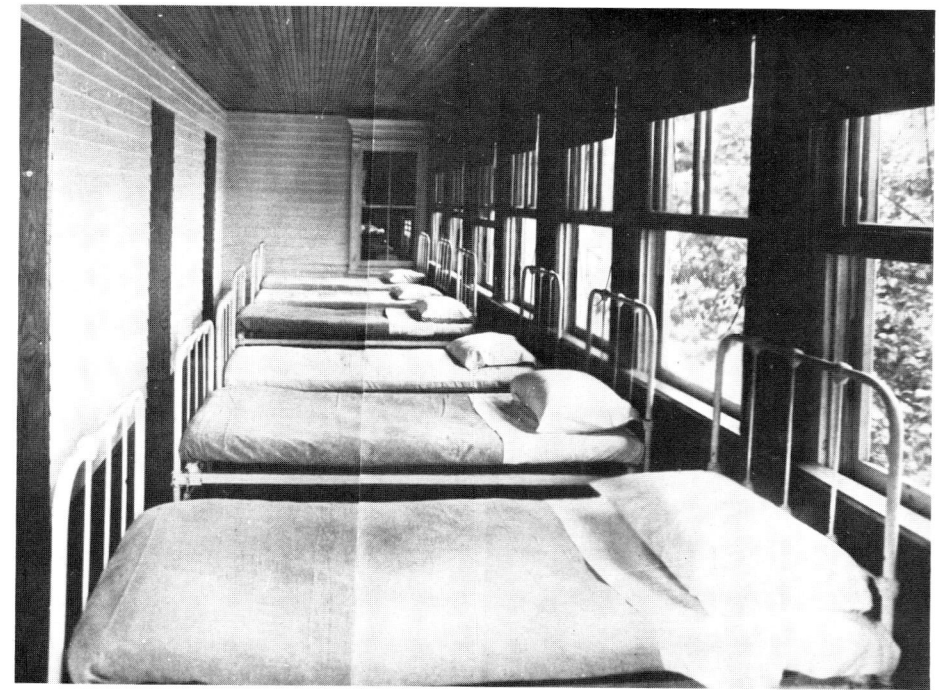

David Totten and his granddaughter Mae Woodruff at his produce stand in New Providence, circa 1912. Photograph courtesy of the New Providence Historical Society

Edward Rockcliffe of Garwood, a plumber and bandmaster of the Aeolian band, stands with one of his grandsons in Garwood. Photograph from A. Van Doren Honeyman's A History of Union County

Battin High School girls' basketball team, 1913-14. Photograph from class of 1914 yearbook; from Charles L. Aquilina's collection

Roselle High School baseball team, 1912. Photograph courtesy of William and Ruth Frolich

Echo Athletic Club, Cranford. Photograph from Cranford, N. J. Illustrated, *1904; courtesy of the Cranford Public Library*

Battin High School football team, 1913. Photograph from the class of 1914 yearbook, Charles L. Aquilina's collection

Children stand in front of the lyceum in New Providence Township, now Berkeley Heights. The lyceum was used for school purposes from 1912 to 1923, when the second floor of the Columbia School was built across the street. Photograph courtesy of Berkeley Heights Historical Society

Only twelve of these eighth graders enjoying their graduation from elementary school in 1916 were graduated from Linden High School four years later. The depression of 1929 changed all that. Because there were no jobs, teenagers stayed in school. Photograph courtesy of the Linden Public Library

The reading room of the Elizabeth Public Library. Photograph from City of Elizabeth-Illustrated, *1889*

Two patrolmen started their daily patrol on bicycles. Photograph courtesy of the Elizabeth Police Department

Elizabeth horse patrol. Photograph courtesy of the Elizabeth Police Department

Plainfield Fire Chief Doane in 1914. Photograph courtesy of the Plainfield Public Library

Engine Company No. 5, Elizabeth, circa 1912. Photograph courtesy of the Elizabeth Fire Museum

Elizabeth firemen posed with the company's cat. Photograph courtesy of the Elizabeth Fire Museum

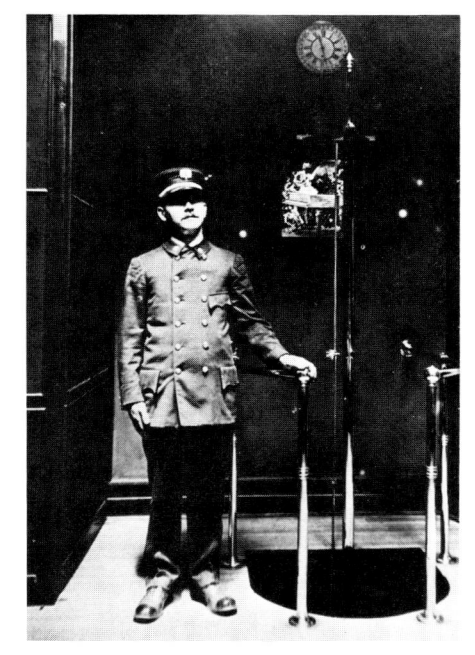

Fireman Fred Clark of Elizabeth, later a battalion chief, stood beside a brass pole. Photograph courtesy of the Elizabeth Fire Museum

The Westfield Town Council was joined by a dog for this official photograph in 1912. Photograph courtesy of the Westfield Historical Society

George C. Tenney, Elizabeth police chief, 1912. Photograph courtesy of the Elizabeth Police Department

Three men enjoyed a ride in Cranford, 1914-15. Photograph courtesy of the Cranford Historical Society

Truck carries new gas stoves. Photograph courtesy of the Elizabethtown Gas Company

Mary Carpenter Woodruff, wife of Noah Woodruff, a Roselle Park butcher, circa 1915. The Woodruff shop was on the site later used by the Roselle Trust Company, Roselle Park. It later became the Roselle Park Office of the National State Bank. Photograph by Sol Young Studios; courtesy of Dorothy Baker

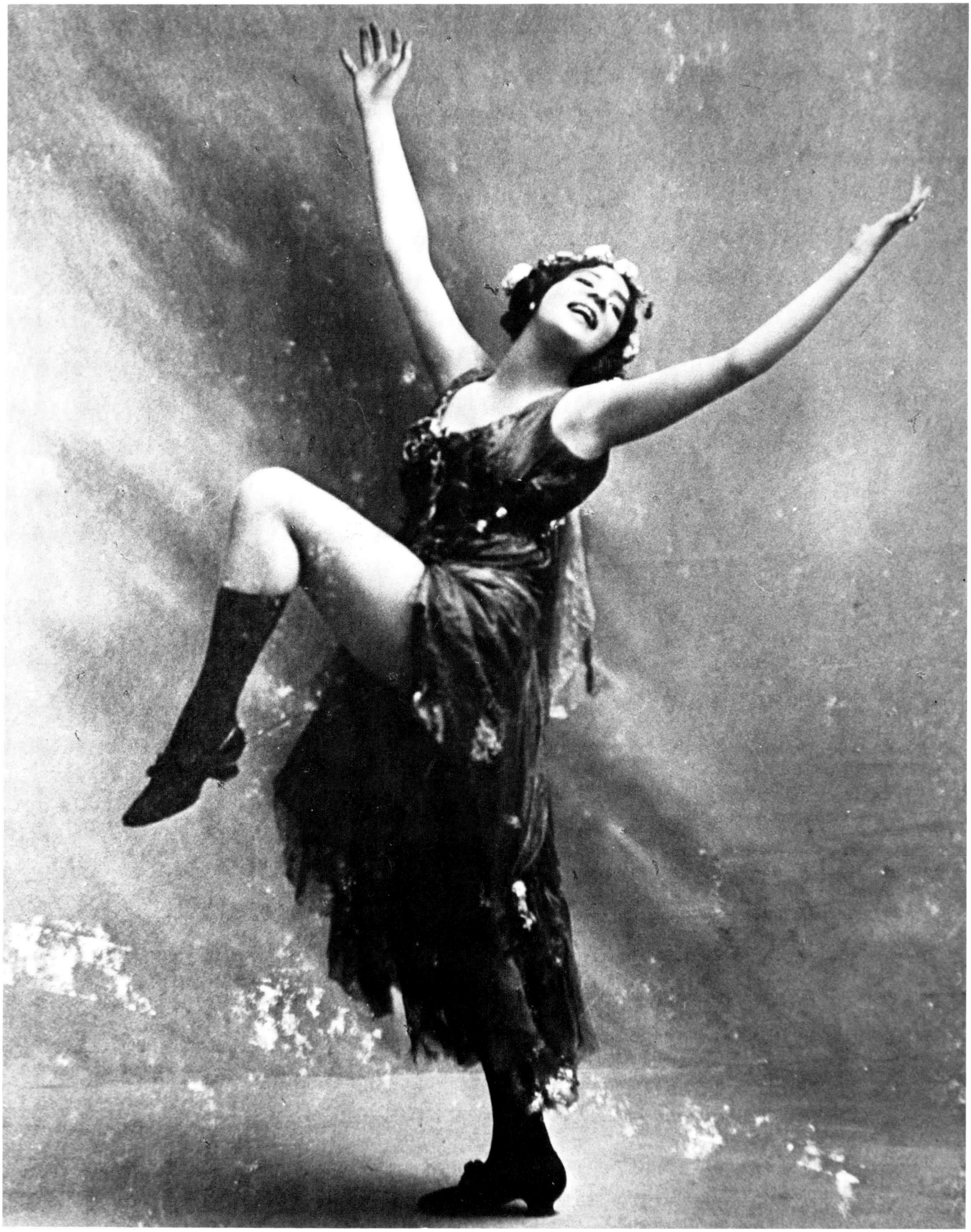

The Blue Dalia danced her way across the stages of Europe and the United States. While touring in the United States, she began writing press releases. After an ankle injury, she became Regina Woody of Elizabeth and began writing children's books and articles. The ballet was one of her favorite topics. Photograph courtesy of Regina Woody

James E. Martine of Plainfield served as United States senator from 1911 to 1917. He was of French descent. Photograph from A. Van Doren Honeyman's A History of Union County

Residence of former Chancellor Benjamin Williamson was used as the Elks' Clubhouse in Elizabeth. Photograph courtesy of the Newark Public Library

James Truslow Adams, historian, resided in Summit from 1901 to 1913. Photograph courtesy of the Summit Public Library

Frank H. Dodd of Dodd, Mead and Company was one of the company founders. He served on the Summit Board of Education and was a member of the Central Presbyterian Church in Summit. Photograph courtesy of the Summit Public Library

173

Fire Chief August Gerstung, first paid chief of the Elizabeth Fire Department, rides in an early fire car. He served from 1902 to 1931. The driver is unknown. Photograph courtesy of the Elizabeth Fire Museum

Big Bill Kennedy was the motorman on the Fifth Street trolley line in Elizabeth. Photograph from the Fiftieth Anniversary Booklet of Division 823, Amalgamated Transit Union, AFL-CIO-CLC, 1968; courtesy of the Roselle Public Library

William Hagin of Elizabeth (standing third from right) was in the American Field Service somewhere in France before America entered the war, 1916. Photograph from a French postcard; courtesy of Dr. Rosa Hagin

Recruits leaving Plainfield railroad station in 1916. Scenes like this were repeated often after the United States entered World War I. Photograph courtesy of the Plainfield Public Library

Westfield soldiers lined up for food somewhere in France during World War I, 1918. Photograph courtesy of the Westfield Historical Society

Guy Bates of Summit, a mechanical engineer, helped to build the Belmont Tunnel under the East River in New York City. He became interested in a refrigerator plant to manufacture and preserve ice. He joined the National Guard of New York in 1904 and served along the Mexican border in 1916, and in France from 1917 to 1918. He was also a member of the Summit City Council. Photograph from A. Van Doren Honeyman's A History of Union County

175

The Lightning Division was composed of several Elizabeth and Union County youths. Photograph from a French postcard; courtesy of Dr. Rosa Hagin

Lieutenant Colonel William B. Martin, an Elizabeth native and dentist, served as a Union County clerk. He joined the National Guard of New Jersey in 1884 and served in the Spanish-American War and in World War I. Photograph from A. Van Doren Honeyman's A History of Union County

Roselle's food committee on August 21, 1917 included: Beulah Gradwehl, domestic science teacher; Mrs. George Harten, chairman of the canning committee; and Mrs. William L. McLaughlin, chairman of the market committee. Photograph courtesy of the Newark Public Library

Philip Marion Drabble, a corporal with the 105th Machine on Battalion, died of pneumonia in Dury-les-Amiens, France. November 5, 1918. Photograph courtesy of the Summit Public Library

Children sold parsley from their war gardens at Roselle's food market on August 21, 1917. Photograph courtesy of the Newark Public Library

The Red Cross workers at the Fanwood railroad station in World War I. Photograph courtesy of the Fanwood Memorial Library

The first submarine for the United States Navy, the S.S. *Holland,* was constructed at Lewis Nixon's Crescent Shipyard, Elizabeth. It was launched on March 17, 1897, and named the *John P. Holland* in honor of the inventor. Several gunboats, cruisers, and other submarines were built at the yards before it was acquired by the Bethlehem Steel Company at the outbreak of World War I. The steel company constructed thirty-four more vessels. After the war, shipbuilding declined.

The Crescent Shipyard. Photograph courtesy of the Elizabeth Public Library

John P. Holland, a native of Ireland. Photograph courtesy of the United States Navy

Launching of the John P. Holland. *Photograph courtesy of Arthur F. Cole*

Arthur Leopold Du Busc served as the manager of the Bethlehem Shipbuilding Corporation in Elizabethport during World War I. He was also employed by the Crescent Shipyard and the New Jersey Dry Dock Company. Photograph from A. Van Doren Honeyman's A History of Union County

Elizabeth's first air crash was in 1919, when the Handly Page airplane built by the Standard Aircraft Company in Bayway crashed. Photograph courtesy of the Newark Public Library

The welcome home celebration in Westfield after World War I featured a flag carried over the "top" by Martin Walberger, a Westfield boy. Photograph courtesy of the Westfield Historical Society

The official welcome home for the Boys of '18 in Elizabeth was held on Saturday, June 21, 1919. Photograph courtesy of the Elizabeth Public Library

Members of the new American Legion Post pose around the Civil War monument in the Fairview Cemetery in Westfield on Memorial Day, 1919. Photograph courtesy of the Westfield Historical Society

The Victory Arch was built in 1919 in Westfield to honor the men who made the supreme sacrifice and served in the "War to end all Wars." It was removed so the present war memorial could be erected in 1923. Photograph courtesy of the Westfield Historical Society

New Jersey Governor Walter Edge shook hands with members of the State Militia Reserve at the dedication of Mindowaskin Park, Westfield, on June 1, 1918. The new park lake was the former Clark's ice pond. Photograph courtesy of the Westfield Historical Society

Station WDY, the first broadcasting station, broadcasted from Roselle Park in 1921. Photograph by Krupel; courtesy of the Roselle Park Historical Society

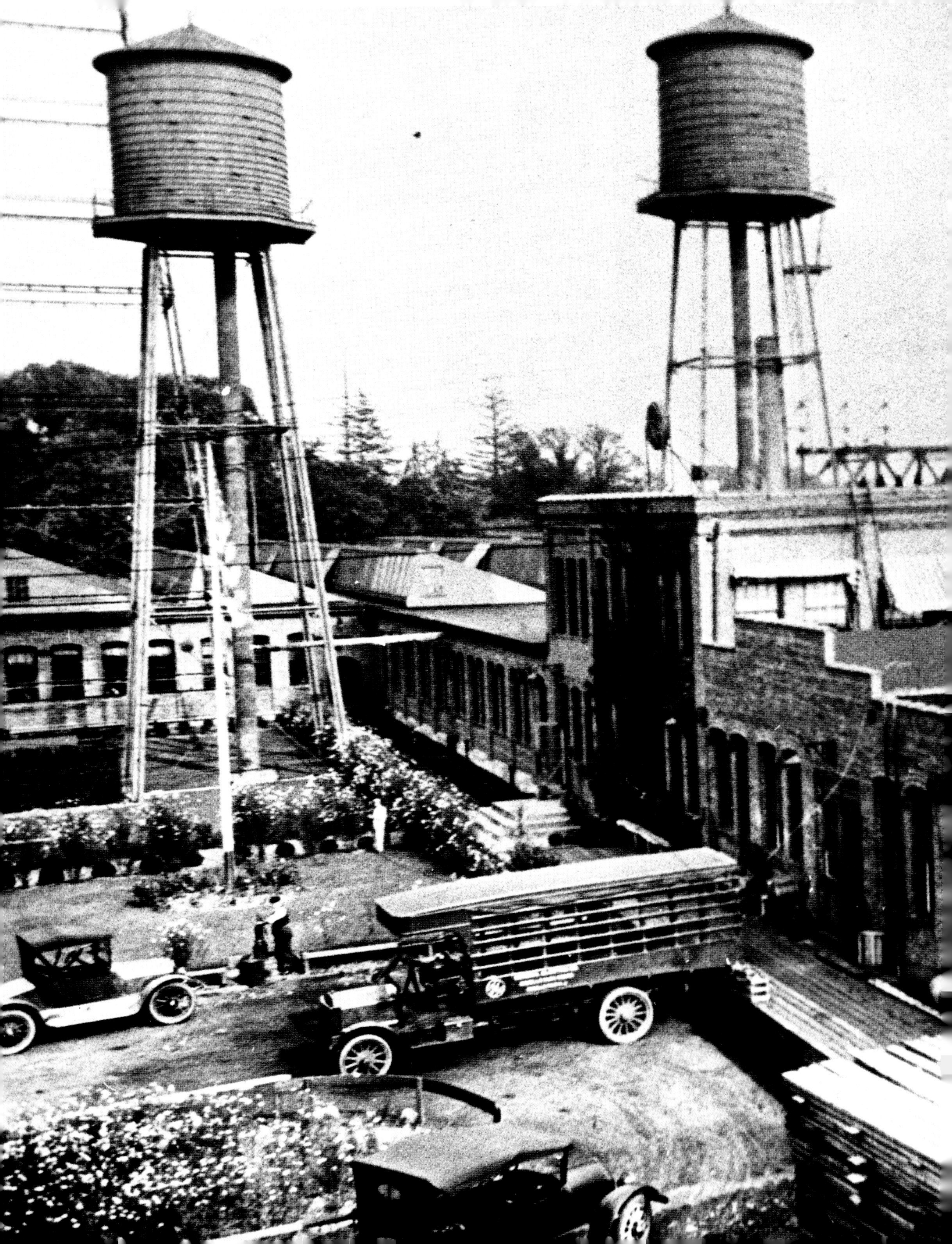

The American Marconi Wireless Company occupied this building from about 1912 until 1919, when the Radio Corporation of America was formed to control it. RCA operated Station WDY at the plant. The initial broadcast was made on December 15, 1921. The station was moved to New York City the following year. It was the first licensed station in New Jersey. The building was used by General Electric Company to make small appliances and by Karagheusian Rug Company to make Guilistan rugs. It currently is occupied by the Romerovski Brothers, recyclers of textiles. Photograph courtesy of the Roselle Park Historical Society

Jazz bands were everywhere. Paul Flammia and His Royal Commanders of Elizabeth thrilled the flappers and brightened the thirties in Elizabeth. Photograph courtesy of the Elizabeth Public Library

The Dowd Pool on the waterfront in Elizabeth was a popular swimming spot circa 1920s. Photograph courtesy of the Newark Public Library

Prohibition took effect January 1, 1920. Poster from Charles L. Aquilina's collection

The "old swimming hole" in the Elizabeth River on the Kean property was a popular spot until it was closed in 1932. Photograph courtesy of the Newark Public Library

Miss Belle practiced what she believed— that women have a duty to the community to improve the quality of life for people less fortunate than they. She was Arabella Halsey Miller. She spearheaded the formation of the Visiting Nurses Association and the Family and Children's Society. She also established the first child health care center in Elizabeth. She turned her family home on East Jersey Street into a private hotel and boarding home and formed the Pioneer Club for youths. The city named the Pioneer Homes in honor of the club. She also was remembered in 1979, when the Arabella Miller Recreation Center was dedicated to her memory. Photograph courtesy of Edward L. Fox

Pioneer Junior Champs in 1924-25. Photograph courtesy of Edward L. Fox

This is probably one of the first aerial photographs of Elizabeth. The Union County Courthouse and the First Presbyterian Church are in the center. The railroad is behind them. Photograph from The Greater Industrial City of Elizabeth. *Picture Supplement, Grassman and Kreh; courtesy of Armand A. Fiorletti*

Aerial view of Pearl and Bridge streets in Elizabeth in 1923. The Elizabeth River curves through the center of the photograph. The Peter Breidt Brewery Company is in the foreground. The pottery works are located beside the river in the center of the photograph. Photograph from The Greater Industrial City of Elizabeth, *1923. Picture Supplement, Grassman and Kreh; courtesy of Armand A. Fiorletti*

View of Broad Street from the Arch, Elizabeth, in 1925. Photograph by J. Fieldman; courtesy of John Doyle

The Union Post Office was housed in John Price's grocery store, circa 1925. Photograph courtesy of the Union Police Department

John Couser poses beside his new Model T Ford in New Providence Township (Berkeley Heights). Photograph courtesy of Berkeley Heights Historical Society

Police Chief Charles Hopkins and family of Union Township stand beside Union's first police car circa 1920s. Photograph courtesy of the Union Police Department

The Eagle's Band, Fraternal Order of Eagles No. 667, Elizabeth. Photograph courtesy of the Elizabeth Public Library

The Fanwood Garden Club about 1928. Photograph courtesy of the Fanwood Memorial Library

Veterans of Foreign Wars, Post No. 184, in front of their post home on Memorial Day, 1926. Photograph courtesy of the Elizabeth Public Library

Andy Young and his bride Monica were the first members of the Pioneer Club to marry. Photograph (circa 1926) courtesy of Edward L. Fox

Mickey Walker, boxer, of Elizabeth. Photograph courtesy of Edward L. Fox

Fred "Red" Cochran, boxer, grew up on the same block as Mickey Walker in Elizabeth. He later lived in Union. Photograph courtesy of Marcel Perret

John Shumate of Elizabeth, basketball star. Photograph courtesy of Edward L. Fox

Jake Wood, 1961, baseball star. Photograph courtesy of Edward L. Fox

Babe Ruth (right), baseball great, is welcomed to a World War II bond rally by Union County detective Frank Bruggy of Elizabeth. Bruggy, who died on April 5, 1959, held the unique distinction of playing professional ball in three sports. He was a star catcher for both Connie Mack's Philadelphia Athletics and Casey Stengel's Philadelphia Phillies, a member of both the Scranton and Syracuse basketball clubs, and played with the Brooklyn Dodgers football team. He later was a big brother to hundreds of Elizabeth youngsters. Photograph courtesy of Dr. Matthew C. McCue

George J. Groh of Hillside stood beside his bus, which he drove from Newark to Elizabeth through Lyon's Farms until 1926, when Public Service Transport purchased the small lines. Photograph courtesy of Henry G. Groh

Trolley and passengers in Union Township. Photograph courtesy of Ada Brunner

An East Coast plane takes off in Elizabeth circa 1919. For a time, it appeared that Elizabeth would handle the mail, but the airport closed. Photograph courtesy of the Newark Public Library

Durant Motor Company built this huge complex on North and Newark avenues to manufacture the Star and Flint motor cars. The company failed to compete with others, and the huge building was closed. On December 1, 1933, it was subdivided as the Waverly Terminal Company and at one time was occupied by forty industries. The Burry Biscuit Company moved into the building in 1935. The company was purchased by Quaker Oats Company in 1962. The S. E. & M. Vernon Company also moved into the building about the same time. It is a subsidiary of Boorum and Pease Company, makers of accounting supplies. Photograph courtesy of the Union County Chamber of Commerce

Michael Redmond equipment was used in this photograph of the Elizabethtown Gas Light Company circa 1920s. Photograph courtesy of the Elizabethtown Gas Company

This gas range was considered to be the model of convenience in the 1920s. Photograph courtesy of the Elizabethtown Gas Company

193

Theodore Hoffman of Hillside was a wheelwright at Phineas Jones and Company, Hillside, in the 1920s. Photograph courtesy of the Hoffman family

Digging a ditch for water on Elizabeth Avenue on August 15, 1919. Photograph from Reverend William F. Kelly's collection

World Wars I and II placed Union County in the forefront in research and development. Dr. John Bardeen, Dr. William Shockley, and Dr. Walter H. Brattain (left to right) received the Nobel Prize in 1956 for their invention of the transistor at Bell Laboratories, Murray Hill. Photograph courtesy of Bell Laboratories

Dr. Arno A. Penzias, director of the Radio Research Laboratory, and Dr. Robert W. Wilson, head of the Radio Physics Department, both at Bell Laboratories, Murray Hill, were named co-recipients of the 1978 Nobel Prize in physics. They shared their award for discoveries of the cosmic background radiation. Photograph courtesy of Bell Laboratories

Ciba-Geigy Corporation, Summit, 1966. Photograph courtesy of Ciba-Geigy Corporation

C. J. Davisson looks at some equipment used in historic measurements of electrons. He shared the 1937 Nobel Prize with G. P. Thomson of England. Davisson's work is part of the foundation for solid-state electronics. Photograph courtesy of Bell Laboratories

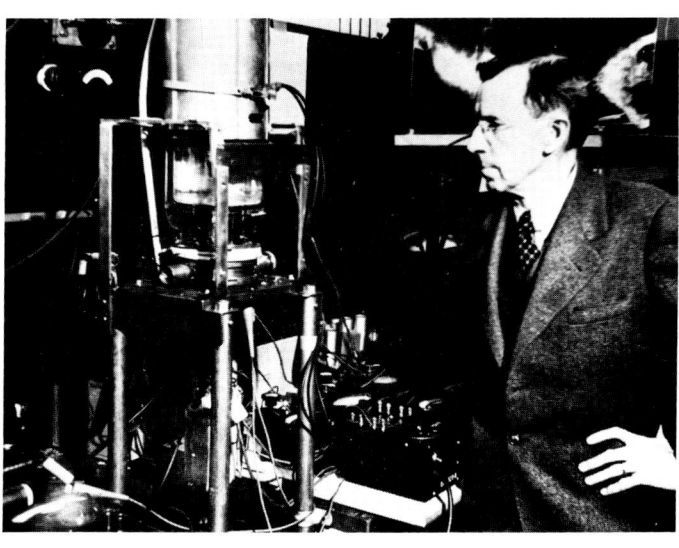

Aerial view (August 1953) of the Celanese Research Laboratories of the Celanese Corporation of America, located in a former junior high school in Summit. Hidden Valley, Union County's newest park, is located behind the building. Photograph courtesy of the Newark Public Library

Edward Reusch of Cranford with the wagon of George Reusch of Cranford circa 1930. The bakery was at Barlow's Corner, South Union Avenue and Chestnut Street, Cranford. Photograph courtesy of the Cranford Historical Society

Burnett's Cider Mill in West Summit (New Providence) in 1927. The mill was purchased by A. L. Burnett in 1876. It was believed to be the oldest cider mill in the state in 1927. It also claimed to make the best cider. There were many cider mills in Union County. Abner Stredt used this building as a tannery before it was converted to a cider mill. It also had been used by Tompkins's feed mill and Walker's wood and block articles. Photograph courtesy of the New Providence Historical Society

Norman and Raymond Stiles, brothers living in Union Township, purchased H. S. Chatfield's Ada Brook Farm on January 30, 1926, for $3,000. The brothers acquired sixteen milk cows, three heifers, one bull, two horses, a milk truck, route and farm implements. These were added to the four family cows. They repaired an old milk house on the Stiles farm and built a new barn. The Stiles Dairy served Union and Elizabeth. Photograph courtesy of the Stiles family

The North Broad Street grade crossing on the Lehigh Valley Railroad, Hillside, September 1926. Photograph courtesy of the Newark Public Library

The Springfield police force, July 1923. Photograph courtesy of the Newark Public Library

Standing in front of a diner in Union Township in 1926 are members of the Union Police Department. Photograph courtesy of the Union Township Police Department

Fire engine, Summit, circa 1920s. Photograph courtesy of the Summit Public Library

The Roselle Park Fire Department, 1920. Photograph courtesy of the Roselle Park Historical Society

Goethals Bridge, now part of the Port Authority of New York and New Jersey facilities, was opened to traffic in 1928, connecting Elizabeth and Union County with Staten Island. Photograph courtesy of the Union County Chamber of Commerce

An aerial view of Act III at Pier 62 in the Port Newark/Port Elizabeth complex on September 21, 1971. World War II caused the seaport area to expand. The introduction of the container ship by Sea-Land in 1962 helped to make Elizabeth one of the largest and biggest containership ports in the world. Photograph courtesy of the Port Authority of New York and New Jersey

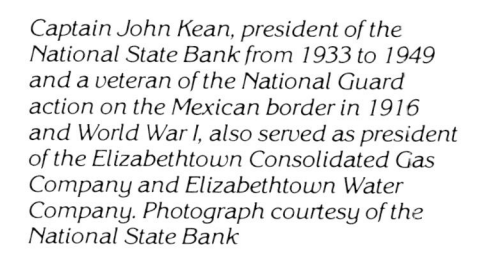

Captain John Kean, president of the National State Bank from 1933 to 1949 and a veteran of the National Guard action on the Mexican border in 1916 and World War I, also served as president of the Elizabethtown Consolidated Gas Company and Elizabethtown Water Company. Photograph courtesy of the National State Bank

U.S. Senator Hamilton Fish Kean, a member of the United States Senate from March 4, 1929 to January 3, 1935, inspected a mule on his farm, Green Lane Farm, Union Township. He was the father of Captain John Kean and the grandfather of New Jersey Governor Thomas Howard Kean. Photograph courtesy of the Newark Public Library

Cows roamed freely at Green Lane Farm when this photograph was taken circa 1935. The former mansion in the background now is the Hamilton Fish Kean Library at Kean College of New Jersey, Union Township. The former Newark State College purchased the estate in 1953 and opened on the grounds in 1958. A multi-purpose institution, it offers a wide diversity of graduate and undergraduate programs to 13,500 full- and part-time students. Until 1969, 99 percent studied teacher training. By 1982 only 25 percent were enrolled in education, and there were more than forty major areas. The college also has purchased the twenty-eight-acre campus of Pingry School in Hillside and is scheduled to use it in 1984. Photograph courtesy of the Newark Public Library

Municipal Building, Garwood. Photograph by Richard T. Koles

201

Scotch Plains Municipal Building, May 1928. Photograph courtesy of the Newark Public Library

Springfield Town Hall, June 24, 1922. Photograph courtesy of the Newark Public Library

Roselle Park Borough Hall. Photograph by Richard T. Koles

Women worked in the field behind a Westminster mansion circa 1937 on the farm of Richard S. Earl, former mayor, in Hillside. Earl, one of the founders of the Hillside National Bank, now the Hillside Office, National State Bank, was Hillside's last farmer. Photograph courtesy of Marion J. Earl

Richard S. Earl, former mayor and former president of the Hillside National Bank, talked with a worker on his farm, Hillside, circa 1937. The farm was the last one in Hillside. Photograph courtesy of Marion J. Earl

Conductors and motormen gathered around an open-air trolley in the trolley yard, Elizabeth, circa 1930s. Photograph courtesy of the Roselle Park Library

Osceola Farms bordered the Rahway River in Cranford. The farms bred and perfected strains of thoroughbred Clydesdale horses and Brown Swiss cattle. The grounds contained a huge dairy barn, apartments, a clubroom for the workers, a dam, and a gristmill. Photograph from the Souvenir Program of the Cranford Carnival; courtesy of Robert J. Fridlington

This aerial view of Winfield Park was taken January 15, 1950. Winfield Park was built on former farm land in 1941 to provide temporary low-cost housing for the employees of the Federal Shipyard at Kearny. The Winfield Mutual Housing Corporation purchased the 700-unit federal housing on December 13, 1950. The corporation continues to own the units and rent them to the residents. The residents, who formed their own township in 1941, have their own township committee, board of education, school, full-time police department, and volunteer fire department. It is one of the most unique townships in the nation. Photograph courtesy of the Newark Public Library

The first electric trolley line to reach Cranford was the Union or Main Line from Newark to Bound Brook, known as "Number Forty-Nine." It was operated by the North Jersey Transit Company. In Cranford cars passed over the Baltimore and Ohio trestle. Many area families enjoyed Sunday outings on the trolley car, riding from one end of the line to the other. In this photograph, taken August 24, 1935, Car No. 2260 passed over the trestle. Less than a month later, buses replaced the trolleys. Photograph courtesy of the Cranford Historical Society

An aerial view of Bell Laboratories in Murray Hill, circa 1950. The laboratories were opened in 1941. Photograph courtesy of Berkeley Heights Historical Society

A new airplane was inspected at the new Linden Airport, September 1942. The airport is owned by the city of Linden. It is one of the few municipally-owned airports in the nation. Photograph courtesy of the Newark Public Library

Women in the Bayway Community Center, Elizabeth, rolled bandages for the American Red Cross in 1944. Photograph courtesy of the Newark Public Library

Thousands cheered when the hometown hero, Admiral William Halsey, a native of Elizabeth, returned home for this parade in 1945. Photograph courtesy of John Doyle

President Harry Truman campaigned for the presidency in Elizabeth on October 7, 1948. His wife's head was turned. At right can be seen Mayor and Mrs. James T. Kirk of Elizabeth. Photograph from Reverend William F. Kelly's collection

Nicholas Murray Butler, president of Columbia University, New York City, a native of Elizabeth, won the Nobel Peace Prize in 1931 for his participation in a movement for international peace. He was the grandson of Reverend Nicholas Murray. Photograph courtesy of Howard Wiseman, executive director of the New Jersey Sons of the American Revolution

Mickey Spillane, the best-selling mystery writer and actor, created the character Mike Hammer both in print and on the silver screen. Mickey was graduated from Theodore Roosevelt Junior High School, class of 1932, and from Thomas Jefferson High School, class of 1936, both in Elizabeth. The photograph was taken in 1948. Photograph courtesy of the Newark Public Library

Adele and Cateau De Leeuw of Plainfield sat with their dog in their home in the city's Sleepy Hollow section. The sisters began telling stories to children in the Plainfield Public Library when they were teenagers. Soon they were writing and illustrating their own books. Miss Adele De Leeuw has written more than seventy books, as well as poems, short stories, and newspaper articles. Her most recent book, dedicated to her late sister, is Remembered With Love: Letters to My Sister. Photograph courtesy of Adele De Leeuw

Charles A. Philhower, supintendent of schools in Westfield, was a recognized authority on the Lenape Indians. He selected the name "Mindowaskin" for the lake and park in Westfield. He wrote many articles about the Indians. Photograph from A. Van Doren Honeyman's A History of Union County

Maxwell Stewart Simpson, Elizabeth native, works in his Scotch Plains carriage house studio, where he has lived for nearly forty years. Photograph courtesy of New Jersey Newsphotos, Inc.

Harry Devlin of Mountainside, also a native of Elizabeth, has never worked a day in his life. After he graduated from college, he decided to paint and write children's books. Some of these he wrote with his wife Wende. Photograph courtesy of New Jersey Newsphotos, Inc.

Barbara Warner Girion, a former teacher at Hillside Avenue School, Hillside, has become a writer of girls' books. Her friend, the former Judy Sussman, an Elizabeth native, now is Judy Blume, also a writer. Photograph courtesy of Barbara Girion

The New Jersey Reformatory (now the New Jersey State Prison) is shown under construction in Rahway in 1950. Additions were being made to an 1900-era building. Photograph courtesy of the Newark Public Library

When F. Edward Biertuempfel (second from right) posed for this photograph with his fellow township committeemen in Union Township, he didn't know that before the year was out he would become mayor. He held the office from 1939, when the photograph was taken, until 1975, when he died, longer than anyone in the township's history. Other members are (from left): Nelson Keib, William Nothnagel, Charles Schramm and (at right of Biertuempfel) Benjamin Romano. Photograph courtesy of the Newark Public Library

Frank Terry of Terry-Lou Zoo walks a llama in front of his home. Photograph by Richard T. Koles

Mrs. Florence P. Dwyer, former congresswoman, discusses retirement. Photograph courtesy of New Jersey Newsphotos, Inc.

A jaguar kitten at Terry-Lou Zoo, Scotch Plains. Photograph by Richard T. Koles

Front page of the now defunct Newark Evening News *announced Elizabeth's third airplane crash in fifty-eight days on February 11, 1952. It was behind the Janet Memorial Home, the orphanage, Elizabeth. Twenty-five passengers and crew members and four residents of an apartment on Salem Avenue were killed.*

Thirty-four passengers and a stewardess survived. Less than three hours later the Port Authority of New York closed the airport. It was reopened November 14, 1952, after it was determined that the port's facilities were not at fault in the crashes. Photograph courtesy of the Elizabeth Fire Museum

Standing at attention during the Memorial Day ceremonies at the Elizabeth City Hall, 1979, were the Gold Star Mothers, whose sons died in World War II, Korea, or Vietnam. Photograph by Richard T. Koles

The explosion on April 21, 1980, on the Elizabeth waterfront at Chemical Control Corporation focused nation-wide attention on the problem of toxic wastes. The company has stored fifty-five-gallon drums containing a cross section of drugs, alcohol, pesticides, insecticides, and many other chemical compounds on the site. The cleanup on the 2.2-acre site officially began in May 1979 and was incomplete three years later. In the meantime, the National Institute of Occupational Safety and Health (NIOSH) was monitoring respiratory problems of police and firemen who fought the fire. This photo was taken on August 3, 1979, three months after the massive cleanup began. In court testimony in 1982, witnesses claimed that while the cleanup was being conducted during the day, additional toxic wastes were being left at the site night. Photograph courtesy of New Jersey Newsphotos, Inc.

Archbishop Iakovos of North and South America (center) prays over holy water, which he sprinkled in the new sanctuary of the Holy Trinity Greek Orthodox Church at Westfield. Photograph (1980) courtesy of Holy Trinity Greek Orthodox Church

The nation's bicentennial gave an impetus toward historical preservation throughout Union County. On these pages are a few of the objects and dwellings that are being preserved.

These old bottles were found in Union County by Earl Brunner of Hillside. Photograph by Richard T. Koles

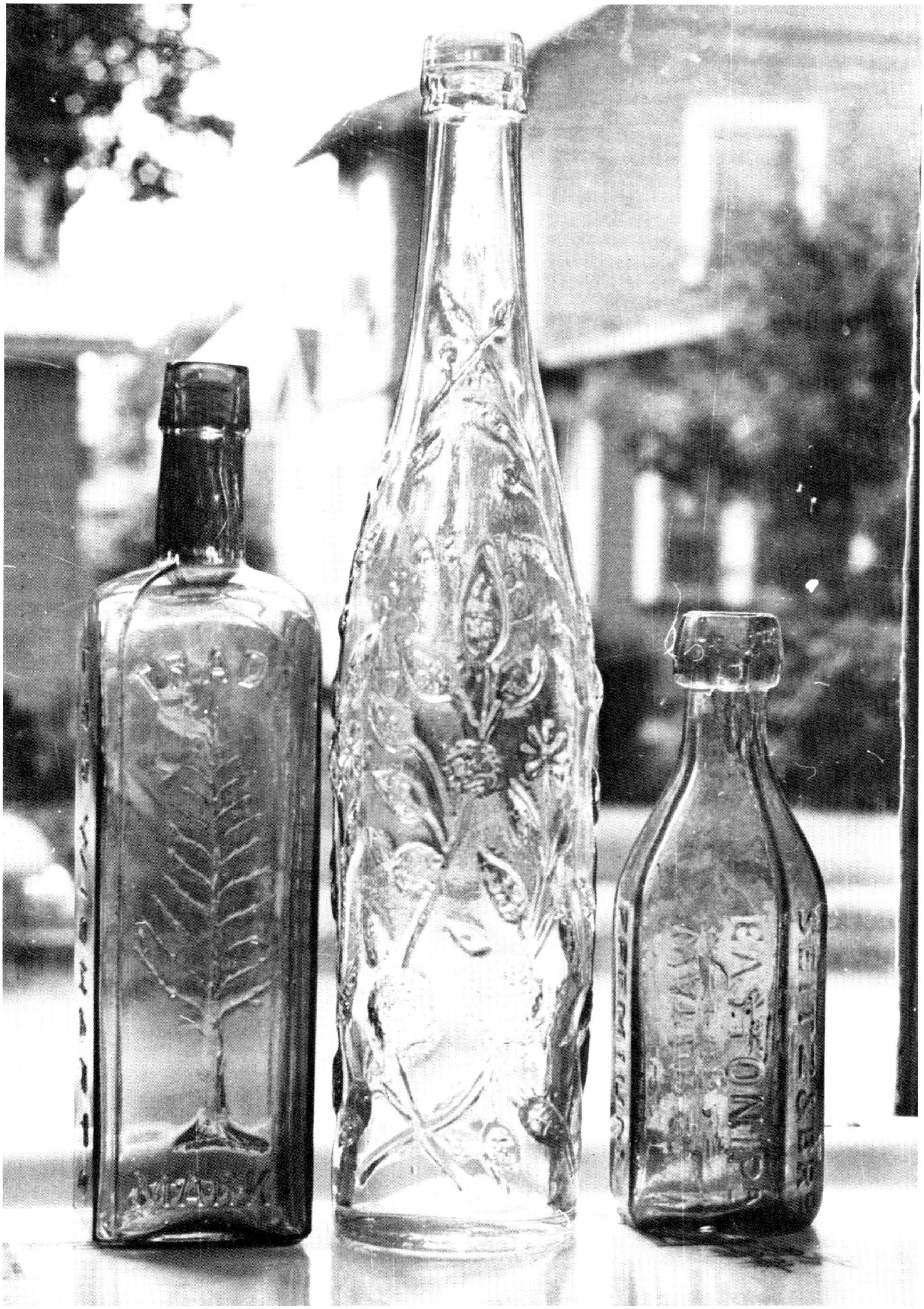

This branding iron belonged to H. W. Crane. From Charles L. Aquilina's collection; photograph by Richard T. Koles

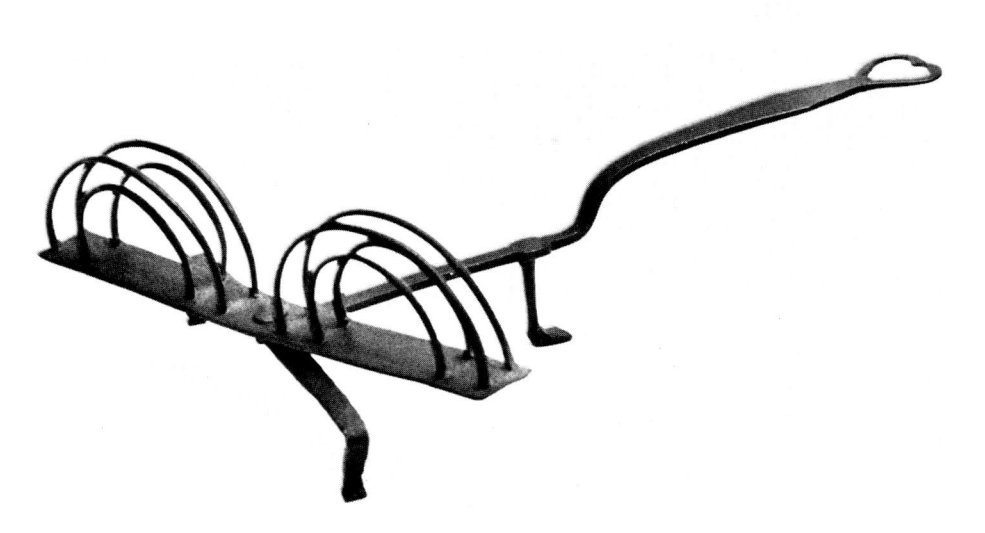

An eighteenth-century toaster from the John Henry Frazee estate. From Charles L. Aquilina's collection; photograph by Richard T. Koles

The New Providence Historical Society's headquarters. Photograph by Charles L. Aquilina

A bicentennial Washington medal. From Charles L. Aquilina's collection; photograph by Richard T. Koles

The Little Lord Farm House is being refurbished by the Berkeley Heights Historical Society. Photograph courtesy of New Jersey Newsphotos, Inc.

ACKNOWLEDGEMENTS

Many people and organizations have helped us to compile this book. Without their aid and interest, the book would have been impossible.

The people include:

John Angelo
Paul L. Angelo
Irene M. Aquilina
Dorothy Baker
Frederick S. Best
Robert Blackwell
Howard J. Bloy
Charles Boll
Cornelia Bowe
Ada Brunner
Bruce A. Buckmaster
Dr. J. J. Butenas
James Clark
Evelyn Kipness Cohen
Arthur F. Cole
Anthony Conte
Carl Corsentino
Charles F. Cummings
Anita Cupo
Don Davidson
Bob Degerhardt
Adele De Leeuw
Tom DiFranco
John Doyle
Kathleen Dunn
Marion J. Earl
Bill Earls
Bertha S. Edwards
Hazel Elks
Alice A. Elmer
Jacob Esocoff
Joseph Famulary
Armand A. Fiorletti
Edward L. Fox
Robert J. Fridlington
John Henry Frazee
Alan Frazer
William and Ruth Frolich
Larry Fuhro
Sally M. Gaetano
Simone Galik
Joseph Gargano
Louis J. Giacona
Barbara Warner Girion
Michael Green
Henry G. Groh
Dr. Rosa Hagin
Walter G. Halpin
Margaret, Richard and Roger Hatfield
Hoffman family
A. P. Kapkowski
Mrs. John Kean
David Keenan
Kathryn Keller
Rev. William F. Kelly
Anthony LaQualia
Perry Leib

Alfred H. Linden
Doris Mann
Barbara Manos
Dr. Matthew C. McCue
Walter Money
Richard S. Mueller
Rev. John F. Murphy
Betty Olson
Frank Orleans
James Osbourn
Dominick Parisi
Clifford M. Peake
Mrs. Edward Pierson
Stephen Pierson
Elizabeth Pisrorik
Carolyn Pryor
Robert Renselaar
A. Carolyn Rice
Patricia Rich
Charles Roll
Leocadia Romel
Dorothy Salter
Melvin D. Shapiro
F. Alexander and Robin J. Shipley
Samuel Stelle Smith
Thomas K. Spear
Elaine Stachowicz
Mary Jane Stiles
Frank Thorne
Florence Traubman
Sara Treat
Police Chief John Truhe of Union Township
Helen Waitkowicz
Howard Wiseman
Regina Woody
Michael Yesenko
Genevieve T. Zagurek

INSTITUTIONS

Alexander Library, Rutgers University, New Brunswick
Bell Laboratories
Berkeley Heights Historical Society
Bristol-Myers Company
Ciba-Geigy Corporation
Clark Historical Society
Clark Public Library
Cranford Historical Society
Cranford Public Library
Elizabeth Fire Museum
Elizabeth Police Department
Elizabeth Public Library
Elizabethtown Gas Company
Elzabethtown Water Company
Exxon Corporation
Fanwood Memorial Library

Hillside Fire Department
Hillside Historical Society
Hillside Public Library
Linden Public Library
Mountainside Public Library
National Archives
National State Bank, Elizabeth
Newark Public Library
New Jersey Historical Society
New Jersey Newsphotos, Inc.
New Jersey Sons of the American Revolution
New Providence Historical Society
Pingry School
Plainfield Public Library
Port Authority of New York and New Jersey
Rahway Historical Society
Rahway Public Library
Roselle Public Library
Roselle Park Historical Society
Scotch Plains Historical Society
Scotch Plains Public Library
Singer Company
Springfield Historical Society
Springfield Public Library
Summit Public Library
Union County Chamber of Commerce
Union Township Chamber of Commerce
Union Township Historical Society
Union Township Police Department
Union Township Public Library
United States Navy
Upsala College Library, East Orange
Westfield Historical Society
Westfield Public Library
YMCA of Eastern Union County

BIBLIOGRAPHY

Allen, Robert. C. *Union Yesterday and Today*. Union Township: Union Township Board of Education, 1962.

Aquilina, Charles L. *June 1780, The Battles for Springfield, N. J.* Elizabeth: Union County Cultural and Heritage Advisory Board, 1979.

Barber, John W. and Howe, Henry. *Historical Collection of N. J.* New Haven: John W. Barber, 1868.

Board of Trade of Elizabeth, N. J. *Old Home Week*, Elizabeth, 1907.

Board of Trade of Elizabeth, N. J. *Old Home Week* 1912.

Burt, George H. *Roselle History*. Roselle Public Library, 1948.

Clark Centennial Committee. *The Historical Review of the Township of Clark*. Clark Township, 1964.

Clayton, W. Woodford. *History of Union and Middlesex Counties, N. J.* Philadelphia: Everts and Pecks, J. B. Lippincott and Co., 1882.

Cranford Kiwanis Club. *Cranford, N. J. Centennial Highlights, 1871-1971*. Cranford, 1971.

Cranford Souvenir Programs of the Cranford River Carnival, 1916, 1962, and 1963. Published by the Cranford River Carnival Committee in 1916, 1962 and 1963 at Cranford.

Cross, Dorothy. *The Indians of New Jersey*, Trenton: Archeological Society of New Jersey, 1958.

Cunningham, Barbara. *The New Jersey Ethnic Experience*. Union City, N. J.: William H. Wise and Co., 1976.

Cunningham, John T. *New Jersey: Mirror of America*. Florham Park: Afton Publishing Co., 1978.

_____. *To Benefit the Whole Population: Union County Park Commission*. Plainfield, 1971.

_____. *New Jersey America's Main Road*. New York: Doubleday and Co., 1966.

Desmond, Helen, ed. *From the Passaic to the Wach Unks: A History of the Township of Berkeley Heights*. Berkeley Heights: Berkeley Heights Historical Society, 1977.

Detwiller, Frederick C. *War In The Countryside*. Scotch Plains: Frederick C. Detwiller, 1977.

Drake, J. Madison. *Historical Sketch of the Revolutionary and Civil Wars*. Elizabeth: Webster Press, 1908.

Ellison, Harry C. *Church of the Founding Fathers of New Jersey*. Cornish, Maine: Carbrook Press, 1964.

Elizabeth Daily Journal. *City of Elizabeth-Illustrated*. Elizabeth, 1889.

Fleming, Thomas. *The Forgotten Victory—The Battles of New Jersey, 1780*. New York: Reader's Digress Press, 1973.

Fridlington, Robert J. *Union County Yesterday*. Westfield: Union County Cultural and Heritage Programs Advisory Board, 1981.

Gale, Joseph. *Eastern Union: The Development of a Jewish Community*. Elizabeth: The Jewish Culture Council of Eastern Union County, 1958.

Hagaman, Adaline. *Early New Jersey*. New York: University Publishing Co., 1964.

Hall, Homer, J. *Three Hundred Years of Crane's Ford*. Cranford Historical Society, 1964.

Hatfield, Rev. Edwin A. *History of Elizabeth, N. J.* New York: Careton and Lanahan, 1868.

Hendrickson, Louie E. *Cranford, N. J. Illustrated*. Cranford: Louie E. Henderickson, 1905.

Hershey, Jean Hesketh. *History of the Borough of Mountainside*. Mountainside: Mountainside Historical Society 1976.

Hicks, J. Maurice. *Roselle, New Jersey: Site of Thomas Alva Edison's First Village Plant*. Roselle: Roselle Historical Society, 1979.

Honeyman, A. Van Doren. *History of Union County, New Jersey, 1664-1923*. Vols. I, II and III. New York and Chicago: Lewis Publishing Co. Inc., 1923.

Johnson, James P. *Westfield: From Settlement to Suburb*. Westfield: Westfield Historical Society, 1977.

Keenan, David L. *Roselle Park: Our Family Album*. Roselle Park: Roselle Park Historical Society, 1976.

Kelly, Frank Bergen. *Historic Elizabeth 1664-1926*. Elizabeth: Sesqui-Centennial Committee, 1926.

_____. *Historic Elizabeth 1664-1932*. Elizabeth: *Elizabeth Daily Journal*, 1932.

Kennedy, John F. *A Nation of Immigrants*. New York: Harper and Row, 1964.

Kobbe, Gustave. *The Central Railroad of New Jersey*. New York: Central Railroad of New Jersey, 1890.

Kosiarski, Mary. *The Regina Music Box*. Rahway: Regina Co., 1975.

Kraft, Herbert C. ed. *Indian Pre-History of New Jersey: A Delaware Indians Symposium*. Harrisburg, Pa.: Pennsylvania Historical Commission, 1974.

Kraus, Michael and Vera. *Family Album for Americans: A Nostalgic Return to the Venturesome Life of America's Yesterdays*. New York: H. W. Wilson Co., 1961.

Lane, Wheaton J. *From Indian Trails to Iron Horse*. Princeton: Princeton University Press, 1939.

League of Women Voters of Linden. *This is Linden*. Linden, 1973.

League of Women Voters of New Providence. *This is New Providence*. New Providece, 1960.

League of Women Voters of Plainfield. *This is Plainfield*. Plainfield, 1972.

League of Women Voters of Springfield. *This is Springfield*. Springfield, 1970.

Lossing, Benson J. *The Pictorial Field-Book of the Revolution*. 2 vols. New York: Harper Brothers, 1850.

Lundin, Leonard. *The Cockpit of the Revolution*. New York: Octagon Books, 1972.

Lyon, A. B. and Lyon, G.W.A. *Lyon Memorial: A Geneology of the Lyon Family*. Detroit: William Graham Co., 1909.

Mayhew, Theodore L. *St. John's Church, Elizabeth, 1706-1981, 275th Anniversary*. Elizabeth: St. John's Church, 1981.

McCormick, Richard P. *New Jersey From Colony to State*. Princeton: D. Van Nostrand, Inc., 1964.

McCoy, John J. *History of the Rahway Valley Railroad*. Kenilworth: Kenilworth Historical Society, 1976.

Meirs, Earl Schenck. *Crossroads of Freedom*. New Brunswick: Rutgers University Press, 1971.

Mellick, Andrew D., Jr. *The Story of An Old Farm*. New Brunswick: Rutgers University Press, 1961.

Unionist-Gazette. Somerville, 1889.

Midtown Elizabeth Directory and Shoppers' Guide. Elizabeth: Midtown Merchants Association, 1981.

Murray, Rev. Nicholas. *Notes Concerning Elizabethtown.* Elizabeth: E. Sanderson, 1844.

Philhower, Charles. "Aboriginal Inhabitants of Union County." *Proceedings of Union County Historical Society.* Elizabeth, 1923.

Pomfret, John E. *The Providence of East Jersey,* Princeton: Princeton University Press, 1962.

Proceedings of the Union County Historical Society. Elizabeth: Union County Historical Society, 1932.

Rawson, Mary N. *Under the Blue Hills.* Scotch Plains: Scotch Plains-Fanwood Historical Society, 1974.

Ricord, Frederick W. *History of Union County.* Newark: East Jersey History Co., 1897.

Shaw, William H. *History of Essex and Hudson Counties—Illustrated.* 2 vols. Philadelphia: Everts and Peck, 1884.

Shipley, F. Alexander and Robin J. and Brandon, Linda A. *Rediscovery of Rahway.* Rahway, 1976.

Smith, Samuel. *History of the Colony of Nova Caesarea of New Jersey.* Burlington, 1765.

Smith, Samuel Stelle. *Winter at Morristown: The Darkest Hour.* Monmouth Beach, N. J.: Philip Freneau Press, 1979.

Thayer, Theodore. *As We Were: The Story of Old Elizabeth.* Elizabeth: The Grassmann Publishing Company Inc., 1964.

_____. *Colonial and Revolutionary Morris County.* Morristown: Morris County Heritage Commission, 1975.

Turner, Jean-Rae. *Along The Upper Road, History of Hillside, N. J.* Hillside: The Hillside Rotary Club, 1977.

Vitale, Charles E., Jr. *Your Town Kenilworth.* Kenilworth: Kenilworth Manufacturers' Association, 1957.

Waitkowicz, Helen. *Pioneer Boys of Elizabeth: 25th Anniversary Program.* Elizabeth, 1947.

Weiss, Harry B. *Life in Early New Jersey.* Princeton: D. Van Nostrand, Inc., 1964.

Winfield Cultural and Heritage Commission. *History of Winfield,* Winfield, 1976.

Woodruff, George Coyne. *History of Hillside.* Hillside: Hurden-Looker Post 50, American Legion and the Hillside Times Publishing Co., 1935.

INDEX

A
Abruzzi Mountains, Italy, 120
Academy Bell, 32
Adams, Judge Frederick, 101
Adams, James Truslow, 173
Aeolian Band, 135
Aeolian Company, 135
African-Americans, 106
African art, 22
African Methodist Episcopal Church, 108
Airplane crashes, 212
Albanese, George J., 121
Alcyone Boat Club, 93
Alexander Library, 82
Alexander, William (Earl of Stirling), 36, 38
American Bible Society, 33
Amodeo, John, 121
Angell, Colonel Israel, 40
Antao, Reverend John S., 128
Apples, 29
Arthur Home for Destitute Boys, 61
Arthur Kill (Achter-Kull), 13, 54, 91
Ashby, William M., 107
Asnon, A. F., 98
Associates, 29

B
Bachman-Veghte Company, 69
Bacivicius, Dr. Antonas, 125
Badgley farmhouse, 20
Badgley, Joseph, 21
Bailey, William F., 92
Baker, Captain John, 14
Baldwin Locomotive Company, 49
Baltusrol Golf Club, 74
Banasiak, Freeholder Blanche, 127
Bannister, J. A., 53
Baptists, 17
Barber, Francis, 14, 105
Bardeen, Dr. John, 105, 195
Bargas, Louis, 129
Baseball, 140
Bates, Guy, 175
Battin, Joseph, 89
Bayly, John, 13
Beerbower, L. B., 52, 66
Beerbower's Pottery, 66
Behre, Charles P., 114
Belcher, Governor Jonathan, 26, 31, 32
Belcher-Ogden Mansion, 26, 31, 32, 50
Bender Academy, 111
Benedictine Sisters, 110
Bercovici, Konrad, 152
"Berg," the, 120
Berkeley Heights, 155
Berkeley Heights Historical Society, 72, 113, 118, 123, 151, 153, 155, 167
Berkeley, Lord John, 14, 17
Best, Frederick S. and Lois, 31
Bethel Methodist Church, 108
Bettman, "Aunt" Carrie, 154
Bicycle club, 85
Biertuempfel, Mayor F. Edward, 210
Bishop, John, 27
Blacks, 9, 106, 108
Bloody Gap, 39
Bloy, Township Clerk Howard J., 154
Blue Dahlia, 172
Blue Mountain Valley, 36, 39
B'nai B'rith, 118
Boehm, George, 98
Bonnel, Jonathan Crane, 59
Bonnel, Nathaniel, 19, 105
Boudinot, Elias, 25, 29, 33, 50, 105
Boudinot, Hannah Stockton (Mrs. Elias), 33
Boudinot Mansion, 33
Bound Creek, 10, 15
Boxwood Hall, 33
Boyd, Charles C., 153
Brachhausen, Gustave Adolph, 60, 146
Bradford, William, 27
Brant, William, 53
Brattain, Dr. Walter H., 195
Bregolato, Reverend Anthony, 123
Breidt, Peter, 114, 187
Broad Street, 98, 136, 160
Brown, Dr. Joseph E., 108
Bristol-Myers Company, 133
Brummer, John, 85

Burlington, 26
Burr, Aaron, Jr., 37, 38, 45
Burry-Lu Corporation, 133, 193
Butenas, Dr. Joseph J., 125
Butler, Dr. Nicholas Murray, 207
Byrne, Governor Brendan, 127

C
Cabot, John, 12, 13
Cabot, Sebastian, 12
Cagney, James, 152
Caldwell, Reverend James, 30, 33, 40, 44
Caldwell, Hannah Ogden, 8, 30, 40, 41
Cannon, Henry R., 110
Carroll, Charles. 150
Carroll, John, 52
Carteret, Lady Elizabeth, 17
Carteret, Lady Elizabeth Smith Lawrence, 17
Carteret, Governor Philip, 9, 14, 16, 17, 25, 103
Cedar Brook, 27
Ceglowski, Walter M., 127
Celanese Corporation, 133
Central Land Improvement Company, 59
Central Railroad of New Jersey, 52
Chandler, Reverend Thomas Bradbury, D. D., 25
Chapman, Gil, 108
Charles II, 13
Chertoff, Rabbi Gershon B., 118
Children's Country Home, 61, 164
Children's Specialized Hospital, 61, 164
Churches
 African Methodist Baptist Church, 108
 Bethel Methodist Church, 108
 Community Methodist Church, 73
 First Presbyterian Church, Cranford, 73
 Holy Trinity Greek Orthodox Church, 131
 Reformed Church, 72
 Scotch Plains Baptist Church, 72
 St. Adalbert's Roman Catholic Church, 126
 St. Anthony of Padua Roman Catholic Church, 123
 St. Augustine's Episcopal Church, 106
 St. Bartholomew Roman Catholic Church, 106
 St. Hedwig's Roman Catholic Church, 126
 St. John's Church, 24, 25
 St. Mary's of the Assumption Roman Catholic Church, Elizabeth, 109
 St. Mary's Roman Catholic Church, Stony Hill, 72
 St. Patrick's Roman Catholic Church, 112
 St. Peter and Paul Roman Catholic Church, 125
Ciba-Geigy Corporation, 195
City Brewery, 109
Clark, Abraham, 34, 35, 36
Clark, Edward, 71
Clark, Fred, 170
Clark, Hamilton, 106
Clark Historical Society, 20
Clark, Richard, 14
Clark, Reverend Samuel A., 25
Claus Bottling Company, 114
Clinton Township, 10
Clinton, Sir Henry, 36
Clio Club, 64
Cochran, Fred "Red," 191
Coe, Russell, 60
Cohan, Zara, 54
Cole, Arthur F., 93, 178
Colelli, Rocco J., 131
Coles, Dr. J. Ackerman, 61
College of New Jersey, 16
Columbia School, 97
Columbus, Christopher statue, 122
Committee of Correspondence, 35
Concessions and agreements, 25
Connecticut Farms, 20, 40
Connecticut Farms, Battle of, 22
Connelly, John S., 109
Connelly, Louise, 155
Connelly Street Railway, 109

220

Conte, Anthony, 121
Continental Congress, 33
Cooper, Harry A., 118
Cornwallis, General Lord Charles, 38
Corsentino, Carl, 121
Couser, John, 188
Cox, William, 81
Crane, "Aunt Betsy" Mulford, 53
Crane, Josiah, 50
Crane, Moses Miller, 9
Crane, Stephen, 35
Crane, Stephen, author, 101
Craneville, 50
Cranford, 10, 27, 50, 51, 62, 73, 131
Cranford Historical Society, 50, 88, 161, 162, 171, 204
Cranford River Carnival, 95, 156
Crater, Warren B., 49
Crawford, William, 152
Crescent Iron Works, 52
Crestlin Boys Club, 124
Cuban-Americans, 129
Cukier, Thomas, 129
Cummings, James, 81
Cummins, Lady Margaret, 27

D
Da Ponte, Lorenzo, 117
Darby, Mayor Elias, 9, 10
Davis, Bernice, 108
Davis, Dr Charles, 77
Davisson, C. J., 196
David, Joseph, 117
Day, Elizabeth Crane, 53
Day's Hill, 9
Dayton, General Elias, 22, 39, 49
Dayton, General Jonathan, 42, 45, 49
D. B. Dunham Carriages, 53
Decker, Charles M., 94
Declaration of Independence, 37
De Hart, John, 35
De Hart, Oscar, 145
Deinlein, Mr. and Mrs. August, 113
Delaware, Lackawanna and Western Railroad, 59
De Leeuw, Adele and Cateau, 207
Dengles, John P., 115
Denk, Harold H. and Jacob F., 114
Denton, Daniel, 13
Detwiller, Frederic C., 39
Devlin, Harry and Wendy, 208
Diamond Hill School, 155
Di Buono, Superior Court Judge V. William, 120
Dickinson, Reverend Jonathan, 15, 20, 24
Diehl Manufacturing Company, 70
Diehl, Philip, 70
Di Francesco, Donald, 121
Dill, Elliot C., Jr., 69
Dimock, A. W., 89
Divident Hill, 15, 18
Dix, J. Augustus, 96
Dodd, Frank H., 173
Dooley, Katy, 91
Doremus, Cliff, 163
Dowd Pool, 184
Doyle, John, 83
Drabble, Philip Marion, 176
Drake, J. Madison, 53, 57
Drew, John, 164
Droescher's Mill, 51
Droescher, Severin R., 51
Dunn, Mayor Thomas G., 102, 109, 112, 125
Durant Motor Company, 193
Dwyer, Representative Florence P., 121

E
Eagle's Band, 189
Earl, Mayor Richard S, 203
Edge, Governor Walter, 181
Edison, Thomas A., 69
Egenolf, Mr. and Mrs. Peter, 89, 90
Electric trolley, 205
E. L. Ewertsen and Sons, 133
Elizabeth, city of, 9
Elizabeth and Somerville Railroad, 52
Elizabeth Daily Journal, 77
Elizabeth Fire Museum, 150, 169, 170, 212
Elizabeth Ice Company, 78
Elizabeth Police Department, 82, 168, 169, 170
Elizabeth Public Library, 11, 39, 43, 79, 91, 157, 160, 168, 179, 189, 190
Elizabeth River, 14, 18, 19
Elizabethport, 10, 11, 50
Elizabeth Pottery Company, 52
Elizabethtown, 10, 15, 18, 29, 35, 50
Elizabethtown Gas Light Company, 67, 68
Elizabethtown Historical Foundation, 31
Eller, Carl, 113
Eller's Grove, 113
Elmer, Alice, 76, 86
Elmer, Rebecca, 161
Elmora, 74
Emmott, Jane, 25
Emmott, Captain John, 25
Esteves, Eugenia, 128
Essex County, 9
Essex and Hudson Gas Company, 68
Ethnic festivals, 112
Exxon Corporation, 142, 144, 169, 170, 212

F
Fabbricatore, Gina, 128
Fair Acres Race Track, 60
Fairview Cemetery, 180
Fajardo, Raphael, Jr., 129
Fanwood, 46, 132, 134, 177, 189
Fanwood Garden Club, 189
Felt, David, 54
Feltville, 54
Ferguson, Herbert, 76
Ferrer, Carlos, 129
Ferries, 10
Fieldman, J., 140, 142
Fiorletti, Armand A., 186, 187
First Mountain, 59
Flammia, Paul, 184
Flappers, 184
Fleacke, Dorothy, 77
Fleming, Thomas, 40
Floyd, Andress, S., 151
Fonseca, Paulo, 128
Foote, Frederick W., 77
Ford, Colonel Jacob, 37
Fox, Edward L., 70, 185, 186, 190, 191
Franklin, Governor William, 34
Frazee, Elizabeth, 137
Frazee, John Henry, 80, 91, 216
Frazee, Mildred, 137
Free Acres, 152
French-Americans, 109
French House, 50
French, Raphael, 42
Fresh Air and Convalescent Home, 61
Friberger Park, 151
Friedman, Benjamin, 50
Fridlington, Robert, 7, 73, 158, 204

Frolich, Ruth and William, 69, 87
Frucht, Mrs. Sigmund, 28
Fulton, Robert, 52

G
Garwood, 135, 165, 201
Garwood Land Improvement Company, 60
Garwood, Samuel, 60
General Motors Corporation, 133
Genova, Rose, 25
George, Henry, Jr., 151
Gerloch, Adam, 113
German-Americans, 113, 114
German-Jews, 118
Gerstung, Fire Chief August, 174
Gessner, Reverend Martin, 12
Gibbons, Thomas, 50
Gibson, Althea, 64
Gidion Ross Farm, 9
Girion, Barbara W., 209
Girl Scout House, 26
Girolama, Pasquale, 25
Gittel family, 62
Goerke, Edmund, 117
Goerke-Kirch Company, 117
Goelthas Bridge, 200
Gold, B. Peter, 118
Gold Star Mothers, 212
Gomel Chesed Hebrew Cemetery Association, 117
Goodman, Bernard L., 118
Gradwehl, Beulah, 175

G
Garwood, 135, 165, 201
Garwood Land Improvement Company, 60
Garwood, Samuel, 60
General Motors Corporation, 133
Genova, Rose, 25
George, Henry, Jr., 151
Gerlock, Adam, 113
German-Americans, 113, 114
German-Jews, 118
Gerstung, Fire Chief August, 174
Gessner, Reverend Martin, 112
Gibbons, Thomas, 50
Gibson, Althea, 64
Gidion Ross Farm, 9
Girion, Barbara W., 209
Girl Scout House, 26
Girolama, Pasquale, 25
Gittel family, 62
Goerke, Edmund, 117
Goerke-Kirch Company, 117
Goethals Bridge, 200
Gold, B. Peter, 118
Gold Star Mothers, 212
Gomel Chesed Hebrew Cemetery Association, 117
Goodman, Bernard L., 118
Gradwehl, Beulah, 175
Grasselli Chemical Company, 60
Grasselli, Thomas, 60
Great Island, 130
Greek festivals, 130, 131
Green Bay, 29
Green, Katherine, 126
Green Lane Farm, 201
Green, Governor Robert, 93
Grier, Mayor Joseph, 93
Groh, Henry, 192
Groh, George J., 192
Grumman, Ichabod, 50
Guerreiro, Joao P., 128
Gural, William, 130

H
Hagin, Julius, 117
Hall, Bolton, 151
Halsey, Admiral William F., 205
Halsted, Benjamin and Mathias, 29
Hamilton, Alexander, 37
Hampton, Andrew, 25
Hampton, Jonathan, 29
Hand, Brigadier General Edward, 40
Handley Page Airplane, 79
Harrison, President Benjamin, 93
Harrison, James, 84
Harten, Mrs. George, 176
Hatfield, Mathias, 14
Hazler, John J., 86, 101
Headley, Leonard, 27
Headleytown, 27
Heins, Harry, 94
Hennessey, Police Chief James E., 110
Hennessy, Michael, 133
Hercek, Halina, 127
Hersh, Louis F, 117
Hersh Tower, 117
Hessians, 39
Hetfield House, 18
Hiberian Volunteer Engine Company No 5, 81
Hidden Valley, 195
Hillside, 15, 125, 133, 194, 203, 209
Hilton, 10
Hinds, James, 27
Hinds, John, 27
Hine, Lewis W., 71
Hobart College, 50
Hobart, Bishop John Henry, 50
Hobart's Gap, 50
Hoffman, Theodore, 198
Holche Yosher Synagogue, 117
Holland, John P., 178
Holmes, Mabel Gertrude, 106
Howe, General Lord William, 38
Hudson, Henry, 13
Hungarian, 130
Hurd, Calvin J., 108

I
Iakovos, Archbishop, 213
Indians, 14, 26, 28, 29
Ingersoll, Charles, 69
Irving, Isabel, 17
Isle of Jersey, 17

J
James, Duke of York 14
Janet Memorial Home, 212
Jaques, Henry, Jr., 27
Jefferson, Thomas, 9
Jersey Blues, 29
Jersey Central Raildoad, 94
Jersey Lightning, 29
Jewish-Americans, 117
Jewish Free Loan Society, 181
Jockey Hollow, 39
John R. Runnels Hospital, 108
Johnson, Thomas P., 103
Jones, Patrolman Charles, 83
Jouet, Cavalier, 41, 43

K
Kanane Buiding, 163
Kanane, John R., 163
Kanane, Surrogate Mary, 163
Kancierius, George, 125
Kanter, MacKinley, 152
Karagheusian Rug Company, 183
Kean, Captain John, 200, 201
Kean College of New Jersey, 75, 129, 201

221

Kean, Colonel John, 77
Kean, Mrs. John, 126
Kean, Peter, 126
Keib, Nelson, 210
Keith, George, 24
Keller, Ernestine, 163
Keller, Kathryn, 163
Keller, Louis, 74
Kellogg, Edward N., 59
Kenilworth, 133, 140, 142, 143
Kenilworth Historical Society, 133, 165
Killian, Victor, 152
Kinch, Dr. Frederick A., 66
Kinch, Police Chief Herbert, 108
King, Rufus, 53
Kinge, Mary, 107
King's Highway, 10
Kiriakatis, Theo, 131
Kirk, Mayor James, 205
Knox, General Henry, 39
Knyphausen, General Wilhelm, 39, 40
Kollock Shepard, printer, 39, 40
Kremser, Edward, 114
Krowicki, Jacob N., 126

L
Lackawanna Railroad, 74
La Corte, Mayor Nicholas J., 121
La Corte, Judge Salvatore Francis, 121, 122
Lafayette, Marquis de, 33, 47
Lakey, Alice, 136
Lambert, Isaac, 80
Larkin, Reverend Thomas B., 111
La Qualia, Anthony, 124
Lattimore, Everett, C., 108
Laucius, Stephanie, 124
Lee, Richard Henry, 50
Lehigh Valley Railroad, 197
Lenape Indians, 14
Leonard, Joseph J., 126
Leslie's Popular Monthly, 41
Lesniak, Assemblyman Raymond, 127
Liberty Hall, 41, 45
Liberty Pole, 31
Lincoln Highway, 134
Lincoln School, 43
Lindberg, Charles, 94
Linden, 43, 61, 72, 95, 126
Linden Airport, 134
Linden Public Library, 195, 155
Lithuanian-Americans, 125
Littell, William, 59
Little Lord Farm House, 217
Livingston, Susan, 126
Livingston, Governor William, 29, 35, 37, 40, 49, 50, 106, 126
Livingston, Mrs. William, 45
Lomack, Dr. Charles, 108
Long, Dennis, 11
Looker, William, 27
Loyalists, 43
Lukacs, Mr. and Mrs. Bela B., 131
Lyon's Farms, 15, 19, 29, 39, 50, 72, 192
Lyon's Farms School, 29, 50

M
Mack, Connie, 19
Mack, (Maskauskas), Simon, 125
Mack, Mayor and Dr. William, 125
Magie Avenue, 99
Magie House, 99
Magie, John, 27
Magietown, 99

Mahan, Admiral Alfred Thayer, 110
Malson, Anne Belle Richards, 106
Malson, Edward G., 106
Malson, Mary, 106
Malson, Sarah Jane, 106
Malson, Totten Smith, 106
Manley, George, 59
Marrow, John C., 85
Marsh, John, 27
Martin, Lieutenant Colonel William B., 45
Martine, Senator James E., 60
Masnicki, Right Reverend Monseigneur Vitus J., 126, 127
Mattano, 14
Mauer, Dr. and Mrs. David, 115
Maurielle, Suzanne Gloria, 124
Maxwell, General William, 40
McCutcheon, Charles W., 59
McDonough, Peter J.,
McKinley School, 147
McLaughlin, Mrs. William L., 176
McManus, Ambrose, 109
Meeker, John, 27
Meeker, John K., Jr., 134
Melyn, Jacob, 103
Memorial Day, 212
Merck and Company, 133
Mercier, Victor, 105
Meyer, Ernest L., 19
Michael Redmond, 193
Middlesex County, 10, 16
Middletown, 26
Millburn, 10
Miller, Arabella, 125, 185
Miller, Aaron, 27
Miller, John (Jake), 83
Millers, 27
Mills, 21, 27, 50, 53, 54, 59
Mill River, 19
Mindowaskin Lake, 208
Monica, Charles M., 120
Montazzoli, Italy, 120
Mooney's Hotel, 135
Mooney, Minnie, 91
Morris County, 10
Morris and Essex Railroad, 59
Morris Turnpike, 10, 31, 40, 57
Morristown, 37
Mountainside, 10
Muhlenberg Hospital, 146
Murnane, Bridget, 112
Murnane, Ruth, 112
Murawski, Edward J., 127
Murphy, Reverend John F., 123
Murray Hill, 114, 162
Murray, Reverend Dr. Nicholas, 207
Musial, Noel, 130

N
Naar, Mayor David, 117
National Cash Register Company, 89
National Institute of Occupational Safety and Health (NIOSH), 213
National State Bank, 45, 77, 109, 203
Naylor, Levi Williams, 74
Nehemiah, Renaldo "Skeets," 108
Neill, Captain Daniel, 36, 37
New Amsterdam, 13
Newark Bay, 70
Newark Evening News, 212
Newark Orphanage, 61
Newark Town, 9, 15, 16, 22, 37, 39, 125
New Brooklyn, 50
New France, 12
New Jersey, College of, 13, 15, 16

New Jersey Journal, 150
New Jersey Railroad, 52
New Jersey Turnpike, 127
New Orange, 140, 142, 147, 150
New Providence, 10, 20, 27, 43, 53, 61, 88, 95, 103, 114, 120, 121, 131, 148, 157, 197, 216
New Providence Road, 20
Nichol, William, 47
Nichols, Governor Richard, 13, 103
Nicols Patent, 29
Niemcewicz, Susan Livingston Kean, 126
Niemcewicz, Count Julian Ursin, 126
Nitsche, Oswald, 113
Nittoli, Dr. Rocco M., 121
Nixon, Lewis,
Nolan, Mrs. Thomas, 91
Nomahegan Lake, 94
Nova Belgii, 13
Nova Caesarea, 15

O
Ogden, Governor Aaron, 45, 50
Ogden, Hannah, 106
Ogden, John, 14, 103
Ogden, Colonel Mathias, 40, 50
Ogden, Moses, 39
Ogden, Robert, 36
O'Hara, George, 50
Ohwath, Zadek, 119
Old Fort, 21
Old Point Road, 39
Old Sow, 40
Old York Road, 9, 10, 28, 47
Olson, Betty, 9
Olympic Park, 9
O'Neill, Joseph, 81
Orange Park, 120
Our Lady of Fatima Roman Catholic Church, 128

P
Paine, Thomas, 37
Painter, Richard, 27
Paist, Dr. Walter and Vera, 155
Parker, Mrs. Roland, 153
Passaic River, 16
Paszkowski, Jennifer, 127
Paternoster, Angelo, 121
Paul F. Korleski Park, 126
Peck, Reverend Jeremiah, 103
Penn, William, 113
Pennsylvania Railroad, 52, 74, 93
Penzias, Dr. Arno A., 195
Perrin, Daniel, 103
Peter Breidt Brewery Company, 109
Peterson, Jerome, 107
Peterstown, 120
Philhower, Charles A., 208
Philip, the, 14, 16
Phineas Jones and Company, 194
Phonographs, 60
Piekarski, Henry Jr., 60
Pierce, David, 16
Pierson, C. C. 159
Pierson, Edward, 107
Pierson, Myrtle, 107
Pike, John, 16
Pingry, Reverend Dr. John F., 75
Pingry School for Boys, 53, 75, 201
Pioneer Boys' Club, 125, 185, 186
Plainfield, 10, 53, 56, 57, 58, 60, 61, 62, 63, 79, 99, 108, 134, 138, 149, 173, 207
Polish-Americans, 126
Polish Falcons, 126
Portuguese-Americans, 128

Potter, Jonathan, 59
Pot Luck, 20
Price, John, grocer, 188
Priesand, Rabbi Sally, 119
Princeton, 20, 33, 126
Prohibition, 185
Proprietors, 16
Pruden, J. M., 66
Pruden, John, 66
Pruden, Keen, 52, 66
Prudential Insurance Company, 91

Q
Quaker Oats Company, 193
Quakers, 15, 72, 103, 106

R
Radio Corporation of America, 183
Railroads, 10, 11, 48, 50, 52, 53, 59
Rajoppi, Joanne, 121
Rahway (Rawack), 10, 11, 16, 26, 27, 35, 42, 43, 50, 53, 59, 83, 108, 113, 133, 138
Rahway Historical Society, 76, 97, 134
Rankin, W. H., 60
Reagan, President Ronald, 129
Regan, Cornelius, 81
Regina Company, 60, 164
Reusch, Edward and George, 195
Rhineland, 113
Riccitelli, Joseph, 120, 121
Riera, James, 59
Rinaldo, Representative Matthew F., 120
Ripley Home, 9
Rising Sun Brewing Company, 115
Ritter, August, 113
Ritter, August, Jr., 113
Roads, 27, 28
Robinson, Dr. William, 20
Rockcliffe, Edward, 165
Rodgers, Captain Marion "Ray," 108
Rodriques, Lucy and Manuel, 128
Rodriques, Councilman Samuel, 129
Roll, Baltus, 63
Roll Family, 148
Romano, Benjamin, 210
Roosevelt, President Theodore, 162
Ropes, E. H., 61
Roselle, 34, 35, 61, 69
Roselle Park, 15, 49, 64, 69, 120, 122, 150, 171, 181, 207
Roselle Park Historical Society, 147, 150, 158, 181, 199
Roselle Public Library, 154, 174
Roselle Trust Company, 165
Russian Revolution, 133

S
Sachar, Edward, 118
Saint George's Avenue, 27
Saint George's Festival, 124
Sampson, Steve, 107
Samptown, 17
Sandy Hook, 13
San Salvador, 129
Santosalo, Thomas, Jr., 120
Sayre Lake, 22
Schering Plough Corporation, 133
Schockley, Dr. William, 195
Schramm, Charles, 210
Schultz, Carl, 115
Schwartz, Bill, 98
Scotch, 104, 109, 134
Scotch Plains, 17, 37, 52, 87
Scot's Plains, 17
Scott, Julian, 53

222

Scott, General and Mrs. Winfield, 52, 55, 56
Scott Park, 114
Seeber Brewing Company, 115
Seeley, Captain Sylvania, 38
Seeley's Paper Mills, 52
Selfmaster Colony, 151
Shady Rest Country Club, 64
Simpson, Maxwell Stewart, 208
Singer, Isaac, 70
Singer Sewing Machine, 70, 71, 133
Sinnott, Surrogate Rose Marie, 121
Slawinski, Reverend Venceslau, 126
Slee, John H., 60
Slomkowski, Edward J., 127
Smith, Samuel, 9, 50
Smith, William Peartree, 35
Smolen, Reverend Joseph A., 127
Soja, John, 126
Spanktown, 16
Spillane, Mickey, 207
Springfield, 9, 10, 51, 57, 61, 111, 121
Springfield, Battle of, 40, 47
Springfield Historical Society, 47
Standard Oil Company of New Jersey, 125, 145
Stanley, Reverend Edward, 112
Staten Island, 36
Stein, Mamie, 133
Stiles Farm and Dairy, 197
Stiles, Norman and Raymond, 197
Stilwell, Mary, 69
Stockton, Hannah, 33
Stone, Charles, 69
Stratmeyer, Edward, 129
Stuart, Gilbert, 45
Stuyvesant, Peter, 13
Summit, 10, 22, 58, 59, 61, 65, 92, 121, 134, 173, 195, 198
Summit Public Library, 173, 176, 198
Surprise Lake, 54
Sussman, Judy Blume, 209
Syers, John, 98

T
Taft, President William Howard, 162
Tallamy, Bertram F., 28
Tanse, Nora, 112
Tappan, Abraham, 16
Tavormina, Carmelo, 121
Taylor, W. Curtis, 45
Temple Beth O'r, 119
Tenney, Police Chief George C., 170
Terry, Frank, 211
Terry, Lou Zoo, 211
Thompson, General William, 36
Thorn, Quillermo, 54, 60, 99
Thorne, Frank, 42, 63
Three-In-One Oil Company, 60
Tip Top Way, 10
Tompkin's Feed Mill, 197
Totten, David, 165
Townley, Richard, 17
Tow Town, 17
Traubman, Mr. and Mrs. Sam, 118
Triarsi family, 121
Trolley, 136, 192, 203, 204
Trotter, William, 105
Truhe, Deputy Police Chief Herbert, Jr., 116
Truhe, Police Captain Herbert, Sr., 116
Truhe, Deputy Police Chief James, 116
Truhe, Police Chief John, 116
Truman, President Harry, 206
Turkey, 103
Turkey Hill, 92

Turner, James, 22
Tuscan Dairy Company, 9
Tweedy, Belle, Florence, Mary and Tiffany, 63

U
Union Aid Society, 53
Union College, 134
Union County, 10
Union County College, 134
Union County Trust Company, 117
Union County Vocational and Technical Institute, 134
Union House Hotel, 46
Union Township, 10
Upsala College, 140, 141
Urban League of Union County, 107
Ursino Lake, 78

W
Wade, Benjamin, 27
Wade's Farms, 27
Wahl, Hannah, 118
Wait, John V., 49
Waite, Mrs. Charles and son, Robert, 158
Waldeck, Reverend Philip, 39
Waldeckers, 39
Walker, Mickey, 191
Warinanco, Indian, 14
Warner, John C., 87
Washington, D. C., 55
Washington, George, General, 22, 28, 35, 36, 37, 40, 45; President-elect, 49; headquarters, 42, 46, 47
Washington, Martha, 45
Watchung Mountains, 10
Watchung Reservation, 54
Watson, Luke, 13
Watts, Reverend Isaac, 40
WDY Radio Station, 181
Weequahic Park, 18
Weltcheck, Harry, 118
Westfield, 10, 20, 21, 51, 52, 60, 61, 64, 65, 68, 82, 84, 85, 91, 96, 101, 134, 136, 137, 161, 162, 170, 179, 180, 181
West Newark, 120
White, Mary Ogden, 65
White, Stanford, 180
White, Reverend Dr. Theodore, 92
Whitehead, Isaac, 27
Whitefield, Reverend George, 29
Whitken, Donald, 118
Wiener, Augustus and William, 86
Wiess, Frank, 105
Wilcox, Captain Cyrus, 84
Wilcox, John, 21
Wilcox, Peter, 21, 26
Wilhelms, Henry, Sr., 113
Williams' Farms, 15, 22
Williamson, Chancellor Benjamin, 173
Williamson, Colonel Mathias, 36; General, 37
Wilson, Dr. Robert W., 195
Winans, John, 14
Winfield, 61
Wiseman, Howard, 96
Wolverson, Peter, 103
Woodbridge Road, 16
Woodbridge Township, 26, 50
Woodruff, Elmer, 84
Woodruff Farms, 15
Woodruff, Mae, 165
Woodruff, Mary Carpenter, 171

Woodruff, Noah, 171
Woody, Regina, 172
Wright, Robert, 27

V
VanDevere, Arthur and Clifford B., 108
Van Pelt, Isaac, 149
Vaughn, Reverend Edward, 24
Vauxhall, 130
Venice of America, 98
Venice of New Jersey, 98
Verrazano Bridge, 13
Verrazano, Giovanni da, 12
Vienna, 105
Viking Field, 141
Visscher, Nicholaus J., 15
Vitale, Carl, 120
Vitale, Charles, 120
Vitale, Louis, 120
Vitale, Paul, 120
Vitale, Sabato, 120
Volunteers, First New Jersey Regiment, 36

Y
YMCA of Eastern Union County, 138, 139
YM-YWHA, 118
York, James, Duke of, 15, 17
York Road, Old, 10

Z
Zagurek, Genevieve J., 126
Zindzius, Reverend Bartholomew, 125
Zouaves, 57

Charles L. Aquilina (left) was born in Italy and attended the public schools in New York. He holds a B.A. in philosophy and history and an M.A. in philosophy from the University of Iowa. Mr. Aquilina has taught in the Elizabeth public schools since 1958 and is presently coordinator of social studies. He has received many awards for his contributions to education, particularly the teaching of history. His previous publications include *Elizabethtown Area Craftsmen, The Capture of His Majesty's Sloop "The Blue Mountain Valley,"* and *June 1780, The Battles for Springfield: A Comparison of Human Interest Accounts.*

A New Jersey native, Richard T. Koles (center) has been a professional photographer for about thirty years. He received his training in photography at the Essex County Vocational and Technical High School, Newark, where he was graduated in 1944. Mr. Koles is a past president of the New Jersey Press Photographers Association and was presented the coveted Bootstrap Award of Region III, National Press Photographers Association, and the President's Medal of the National Press Photographers Association. He either photographed or copied photographs for *Elizabethtown and Union County: A Pictorial History.*

Jean-Rae Turner (right), also a New Jersey native, has been a professional writer for thirty-six years. She majored in history and English at Trenton State College and received her master's degree in the teaching of history at Teachers' College, Columbia University. She has written for the *Daily Journal,* Elizabeth, and the *Community Paper,* Elizabeth, and is currently affiliated with the public information office of Kean College. In 1967 she was named Woman of the Year by the New Jersey Daily Newspaper Woman's Association. She was awarded the Hillside Lodge, B'nai B'rith Americanism citation in 1979 for writing *Along the Upper Road, a History of Hillside, N.J.* Ms. Turner also has received numerous citations from community groups for a wide variety of stories that she has written as well as for her efforts on behalf of youth in the community.

Map of U

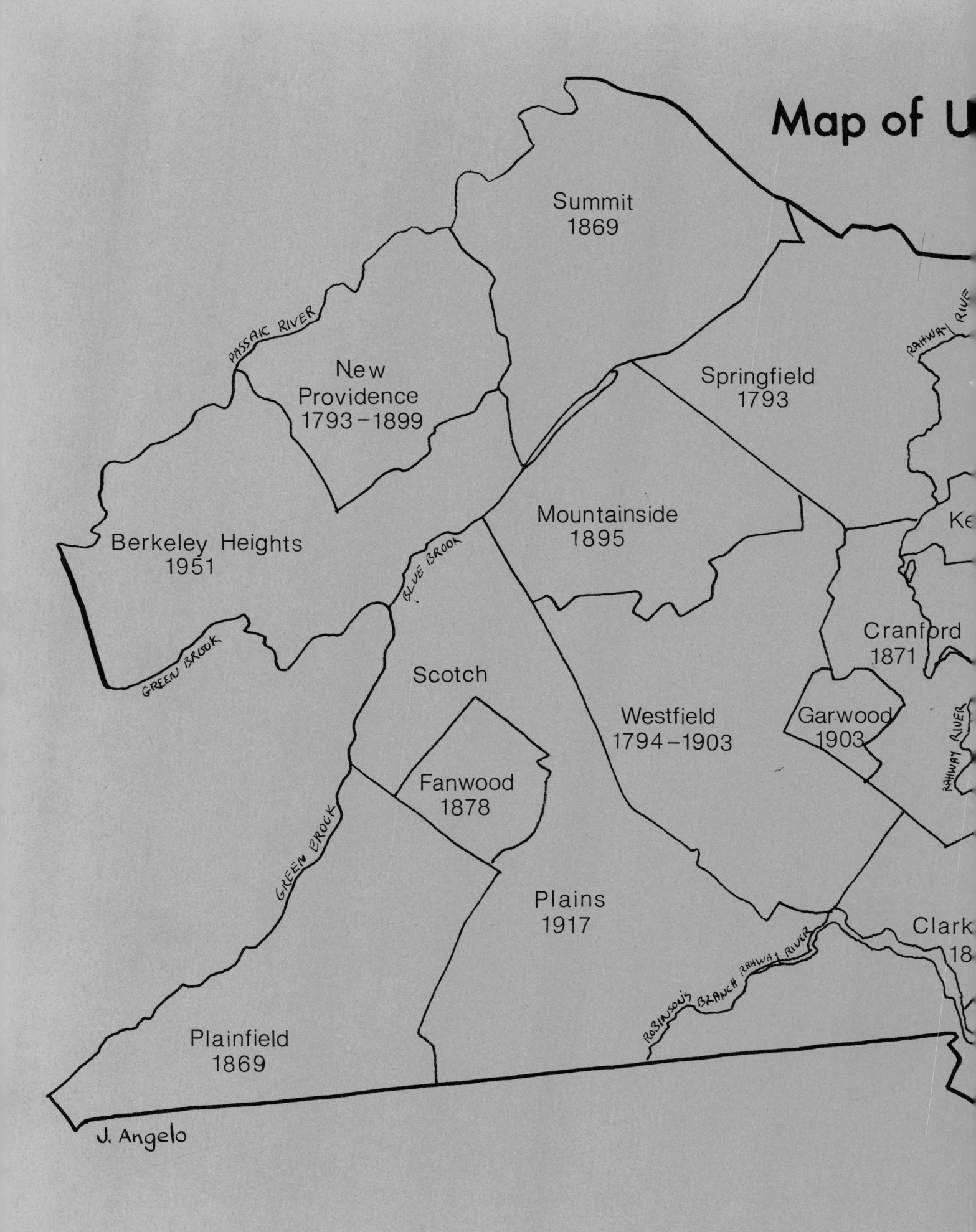

Summit 1869

New Providence 1793–1899

PASSAIC RIVER

Springfield 1793

RAHWAY RIVER

Berkeley Heights 1951

BLUE BROOK

Mountainside 1895

Ke

GREEN BROOK

Scotch

Westfield 1794–1903

Cranford 1871

Garwood 1903

RAHWAY RIVER

Fanwood 1878

GREEN BROOK

Plains 1917

Clark 18

ROBINSON'S BRANCH RAHWAY RIVER

Plainfield 1869

J. Angelo